WRITING IT DOWN FOR JAMES

WRITING IT DOWN FOR JAMES

Writers on Life and Craft

EDITED BY KURT BROWN

BEACON PRESS
BOSTON

Beacon Press
25 Beacon Street
Boston, Massachusetts 02108-2892
www.beacon.org

Beacon Press books
are published under the auspices of
the Unitarian Universalist Association of Congregations.

First digital-print edition 2001

Royalties for this publication accrue to the benefit of Writers' Conferences and Festivals, a national organization of conference directors.

Library of Congress Cataloging-in-Publication Data
Writing it down for James : writers on life and craft / edited by Kurt Brown.
p.   cm.
ISBN 0-8070-6349-5
1. American literature—20th century—History and criticism—Theory, etc.   2. Authors, American—20th century—Biography.   3. Authorship.   I. Brown, Kurt.
PS225.W73   1995
810.9´005—dc20   93-40635

CONTENTS

PREFACE

This is the second annual edition in our *Writers on Life and Craft* series. Each year, hundreds of lectures are given at writers' conferences and festivals across the country. We select those outstanding for quality, style, perspective, and scope. We believe the concept of "craft" has been too narrowly defined, and that a broader definition is needed. Consequently, the lectures we have chosen speak of more than setting or plot, timing, imagery, formal strategies, overall technique, or painstaking considerations of how and where to break a line. Rather, we assume these as part of a writer's apprenticeship, and look for mature work, work whose craft is focused on subject, thought – a whole approach to literature and life.

Any group of writings collected from such various sources is bound to be diverse, and not cohesive as to subject or theme. Still, by some natural principle of selection whose workings are unknown to us, a group of lectures will often exhibit something like a motif, an idea that flits in and out of various writings as if its time had come and a number of different writers in different places across the country had begun to think of it almost simultaneously. This year that subject is travel. Whether psychologically or geographically, into outer space – as in Gary Paul Nabhan's "The Far Outside" or Pattiann Rogers's meditations on cosmology – or inner space – as in Bruce Duffy's imaginative reconstruction of the life of Wittgenstein or M. Nourbese Philip's self-questioning search for Sycorax and the true identity of the Caribbean soul. Sometimes, as in John Malcolm Brinnin's urbane account of various jaunts, travel is quite literal, requiring a steamer trunk and passport. David Wojahn and Lynda Hull even remind us of the risks of travel for the writer – not physical, but ethical and moral.

Many of these lectures have been given at more than one conference or festival. They are attributed here to the program whose director submitted them for consideration in this book. Without the cooperation and support of directors, who are in the best position to assess and garner fine lectures, such an offering as this would be impossible to compile. We thank them for their efforts, and the efforts of those whose submissions were, for one reason or another, not selected. Such effort is not wasted, but represents a potential that might not otherwise have existed, for both reader and writer. Meanwhile, we invite you to set forth among these writings with an inquiring and open mind. "Complex things," Hull and Wojahn explain, "set us voyaging."

Bon voyage!

Kurt Brown
Executive Director, Writers' Conferences and Festivals
October, 1993

WRITING IT DOWN FOR JAMES

JOHN MALCOLM BRINNIN

Travel and the Sense of Wonder

[KEY WEST LITERARY SEMINAR]

Space-age technologists tell us that we are the first people for whom it is possible to possess any corner of the globe within twenty-four hours – the first travelers for whom the fourth dimension is not a mere hypothesis but an available experience. This very afternoon, you or I could leave the White Sands Missile Range or the Houston Space Center and, tomorrow, be set down in some vestigial pocket of the Stone Age. Bucketed beyond the sound barrier, we could arrive at a place where existence depends on crude tools and weapons, and enter a time still innocent of chronology. Yet what we can do, literally, is but a demonstration of what, figuratively, writers have always done. From Marco Polo's pictures of a brutish territory not yet called Siberia to Jan Morris's descriptions of the terraced promenades of Simla, we have seen how imagination can turn a location into an event and fix it permanently into consciousness. In that process, the carelessness of time is brought to account, arrested for moments the sum of which we call history.

Notions like these have led me to my theme: the role of a sense of wonder in the impulse to travel and then in the enterprise of travel writing. I would like to think that this sense is essential; but I know it is not. Some of the soupiest travel writing on record has been done by moonstruck impressionists aspiring to literature; some of the best by close observers aiming to convey no more than pertinent information, a credible economic or sociological overview, a guidebook devoid of Chamber of Commerce soufflé.

Yet you know as well as I that great travel writing is suffused by a sense of wonder as compelling as it is elusive. A phenomenon that cannot be conclusively defined, it remains best comprehended by its effects. Of these, the most constant is the way in which a sense of wonder discloses a capacity for wonder impervious to its opportunities. A great narrative of travel is the product of a writer for whom the given subject is but a convenient focus — a chance to draw upon a personal vision that exists before and after any number of its adventitious expressions. Unfortunately, a sense of wonder cannot be instilled, installed, or otherwise attained. Rather it is something like a musical sense — if not quite a matter of absolute pitch, a disposition, something in the genes as exempt from judgment as the incidence of brown eyes or blue. When it's there, its presence is indubitable; when it's absent, it's not likely to be missed. But even individuals without a flick of wonder can respond to its perceptions and, sometimes, its audacity.

Not long ago, when the now hapless city of Beirut was the so-called Paris of the Middle East, I spent a few days there — one of them on an excursion to Baalbek to see the great temple of the sun associated with its ancient name, Heliopolis. The trip was made in a car shared with strangers and a Lebanese driver. When our visit to the gigantic ruins was over, we squeezed back into our seats in a stunned silence that seemed the only appropriate response to such overwhelming magnificence. This spell lasted for many miles, broken, finally, by the muffled syllables with which each of us tried to describe the indescribable. The only one who did not open her mouth was a well-upholstered woman of sixty — until, that is, she was quite ready to speak her mind. "What I want to know," she said, "is how American Express *finds* these places."

Whatever else it is, the sense of wonder is both contingent and dependent. Since it cannot translate itself, it must, professionally speaking, call upon another faculty of equal importance. That faculty may be called the spirit of investigation. Whereas wonder is a state of receptivity that simply widens or contracts in response to stimuli, the spirit of investigation is active, charged with curiosity, avid to know how and why things come to be, how they work, to what they may be compared, how they fit into any scheme that may render them comprehensible. It is a spirit concerned with otherness, something beside and beyond that can be translated, first for love and then for as much cold cash as may be extracted from the editors of glossy journals. Functioning at its best, the spirit of investigation relates the observer to the observed, makes the exotic familiar, and dismantles those mysteries wonder would as soon keep to itself. By description, measurement, and statistics, the spirit of investigation confirms what my generation knows as "the ineluctable modality of the visible" and so completes an equation in which the sense of wonder can get off its aspirations and go to work.

What might appear to be a philosophical or, at least, a temperamental disparity challenges the writer to unite a subjective musing with objective evidence, to connect the poetry with the prose and so nudge travel writing away from its current status as a consumer report onto the threshold of a literary genre.

As any professional will tell you, among its benefactions, travel is most generous with the gift of serendipity. And since all travel writing is, inescapably, a form of autobiography, I'd like to cite a few instances, a few serendipitous moments when, indulging my own sense of wonder and driven by the spirit of investigation, I tried to find, or make, a balance that would justify my pretensions to a place somewhere in the vicinity of those writers whose chronicles of travel experience I most admire.

Of all the images that passed before my eyes in midchildhood, two affected me like summonses. One was a colored illustration on the cover of a geography book of the young Christopher Columbus, richly dressed in quattrocento velvet, gazing westward from a deepwater dock in Genoa. There, I thought, was a boy no older than I who, just like me, had the whole world in his head and still looked forward to another. The second was a painting of what seemed to me a celestial city. Situated at the conjunction of a river and an ocean, it was the scene of dazzling energy as flotillas of ships steamed in and out, railroad trains snaked across lacework bridges, and airplanes with open cockpits soared above steeples and tall smokestacks. I knew at first glance I had seen the city of my dreams. The fact that it would turn out to be New London, Connecticut – New London! – did nothing to diminish that first impression. Whenever I'm in New London, and that is often, I simply paste my old fantasy over its reality and go on my way.

At the age of nineteen, after what already seemed a lifetime besotted with Europe and the westward march of civilization that, of course, culminated in my birth, I'd saved up enough money from clerking in a bookstore and caddying at a country club to embark on a transatlantic voyage. My bewildered father drove me to the train station and there, shaking his head and my hand at once, saw me off to New York, quite unaware that the figure in the day coach window who waved back was not his only son but Christopher Columbus in reverse and, as far as I was concerned, in velvet. Every night of that voyage – the first eastward crossing of the *Queen Mary* – would find me strolling on deck, humming with the wind in the rigging, or singing aloud a popular song, "With My Eyes Wide Open I'm Dreaming." As we were about to come to landfall, I was so deeply in thrall to what was happening I could neither eat nor sleep nor do anything but dream the imminent horizon into actuality. And then one morning, through a scrim of mist, or tears, there it was – the pale green coast of France. No one had told me lies, it's all true, I thought: Europe exists. In that same moment, eyes wide open, I was hit with a second emotion – a surrender of all my castles, a divestment of illusions I alone could support, and I was ready to go home, to retreat into the comfort of contemplation rather than to hazard all that was waiting for me. In one moment of divine confusion, I had learned that wonder exists before and after any encounter that might verify its premises or resist its promiscuous embrace.

My involvement with travel writing came late but started early – in those years of the twenties when the word *picturesque* was still acceptable in polite society and before it had plunged into the pejorative from which it would never emerge. Apprenticed to the picturesque, I became its victim but only until, at the age of twelve, I learned to spit, use bad words, and otherwise keep my mouth shut. As far as travel writing was concerned, elected silence kept me clean and inoffensive for another forty years. Then some dormant but incorrigible impulse led me to try my hand once more.

Paging through *Time* one evening, I turned to my companion. "Here's something I want to know all about," I said. "What's that?" "It seems the Cunard people are building a new ship – a superliner to replace the *Queen Mary* and *Queen Elizabeth*." The stare I got was blank. I had only recently given up the idea of going to Ararat to investigate the historical sources of Noah's Ark. Next day I called my agent. This man knew me only as a literary type – one of those who wrote poetry and criticism and the occasional biography; in other words, one of those charity cases some agents take on to give their questionable operations a touch of respectability.

"Let me get this straight," he said. "You want to do an article on a boat that doesn't exist." "That's right," I told him. "See if you can get me a commission – something that will put me behind the scenes. I need entrée."

Some eighteen months later, my commission executed, I found myself in Glasgow. I had meanwhile personally supervised the progress of the *Q4*, as the unnamed *Queen Elizabeth 2* was then called, from her beginnings as a skeletal maze of steel to the handsome black hull and white superstructure now towering above the tallest gantries of John Brown's Shipyard. There was no one – architect, decorator, navigator, or engineer – I had not come to know, not a detail of her construction I had not studied, not a representative swatch of fabric or saucer of Wedgwood I had not held in my hands. Now it was the eve of a declared holiday when the already famous last of the liners was to be christened and launched by the queen herself, with Prince Philip and Princess Margaret in attendance.

Caught up in the spirit of things, I had hired a car – a Daimler Saloon Car so big you could stand up in it – and the Glaswegian chauffeur who came with the deal. To get to Clydeside and the launching ceremony early, I'd asked the driver to meet me at the entrance to the hotel at nine. And there he was, having taken it upon himself to decorate the car with hankie-sized Union Jacks and a pennant that looked suspiciously like a royal standard. But in this I was mistaken. My Daimler was not the festooned Daimler but the one parked beside it. The decorated Daimler was Princess Margaret's, ready to take her to a rendezvous with her sister and brother-in-law in some part of the shipyard. Off we went on the seven-or-eight-mile journey – I with my press pass securely in hand, but wondering how I might get my obliging driver into the stands reserved for what the British call "the quality." As we approached Clydeside, people began to line both sides of the road, many of them schoolchildren who'd been given the day off. When the roadsides through which we passed were so crowded as to become a kind of tunnel of expectation, the bystanders began to wave their flags and shout out greetings. Helplessly exposed in my glass cage, I tended to shrink from these displays of untoward interest; but it wasn't long before I caught myself waving back – in that noticeably diffident noblesse oblige I'd seen in TV close-ups of royal processions. By the time we were in sight of the shipyard's great iron gates, the cheers were raucous and I had lost all control. Both hands in the air, turning from side to side, I blessed them all as the gates swung open and we sailed through, home free. "How did you bring that off?" the driver called back. "Trust me," I said, and on we went to watch the great ship go sliding on tons of grease into the waters of the River Clyde.

Holiday was the most illustrious magazine of its kind in those years; and when my article on the new Cunard flagship appeared there, quickly followed by requests for similar pieces from the *New York Times* and the *Atlantic Monthly* and a long-term assignment from the *New Yorker*, I knew I had been blooded, initiated into the excitement of travel-with-a-purpose and into its quicksilver realm of serendipity. Research had led me into so many unexpected byways and untouched archives that I had come to a point of no return and a new role – as a sort of Grandpa Moses of maritime history. The book I produced some five years later was called *The Sway of the Grand Saloon: A Social History of the North Atlantic*. Its theme is ocean liners as metaphorical reflections of social change in Europe and America from the first scheduled sailing of a clipper ship in 1819 to the final crossing of the *Queen Mary* in 1967. Its subtheme is a propensity for mythmaking by which a rivets-and-bolts industry became a popular romance.

A sense of wonder, finding its voice in the spirit of investigation, had forged a document that – however minor in the large account – has remained unique. The wharf-rat kid who'd hung around the ocean terminals of Halifax and the decaying piers of Boston for half of his young life had turned an obsession into a career. Other books would follow; but now that mini career is over – by choice, and under the late-arriving conviction that travel writing per se is a fictitious category of nonetheless unlimited opportunity.

Out of a thousand disjunct recollections of seaborne questing, two particular encounters continue to remind me that – compared with souls transfigured by a determination to seize as much of the world as their means would allow and their grasp contain – I remain an impulsive dabbler in a realm of apprehension where, as far as they are concerned, wonders never cease.

One of these was a little man whose name I never knew but who haunts my memory as he once dogged my footsteps. I describe him as "little" with no invidious intent, but merely to suggest that his meek address and mute pathos gave him the air of a reference looking for a subject. Summer after summer, I'd spot him on the edge of a crowd – once in Scotland, once in Trieste, once between the acts of an opera in Odessa. Dressed in the same neat blue suit and clutching a shapeless sort of reticule, he was always alone and almost, but not quite, smiling. Was he, time and again, the same man, I wondered? Or was he but the manifestation of a type? "There he is again," I said to a companion who knew me well enough to catch at once what I meant. We had just boarded a motor coach in Palermo on which we would crisscross Sicily to visit its Roman and Greek sites. In the course of the following week, we met his perpetual half-smile with smiles of our own and one afternoon, at a streetside café, sat at a table with him long enough to learn that he for many years held a desk job with the Department of the Navy, had retired at the age of fifty, and now "just liked to travel." A few days later, established for a time in Taormina, I was reading a newspaper in its little plateau of a piazza in front of the cathedral when a wedding party came spilling out of its tall doors in a blur of veils, flowers, and the salutations of a retinue of guests – among them the little man. There was a daisy in the lapel of his blue suit and when he reached into his grungy bag, out came handfuls of rice with which he showered the wedding party on its way to an ancient limousine. When the bride and groom were about to be driven away, he stepped out through the crowd, blew them a kiss, and retreated to a point a few feet from where, unnoticed by him, I sat with my newspaper. "Relatives of yours?" I asked. "No." "Friends?" "No." A long pause. "Oh, I go to everything," he said, "christenings, funerals, weddings. I love to see life happening."

Put to shame on the spot – a spot from which I'm not sure I've ever moved – I like to think that, somewhere along his solitary way, that little man became a bona fide member of somebody's wedding, that somewhere he crashed a banquet, only to find his name on a place card beside his own wine glass, and even that he gets a postcard, out of the blue now and then, saying "Wish you were here."

My other memory is as glad as the circumstance on which it's based and the heresy it has served to correct. In the grip of one of the many misapprehensions that attend advancing age, I'd quite convinced myself that, however many acquaintances one might accumulate, no one ever, ever, makes an intimate friend beyond the age of fifty. Then along came disproof incarnate.

Rita was the only daughter of an Armenian who had become a British subject long before she was born on a fashionable edge of Hyde Park. To suggest the degree of comfort in which she spent her infancy and the source of an intractable shyness she never overcame, let me quote some uncharacteristically purple prose from the *New Yorker* in which her father is described as "that shadowy Armenian gentleman whose vast holdings include five per cent of the oil in Iraq and who, at his death, was widely regarded as the world's wealthiest private citizen and we had heard tales of how abrupt silences descended on international conferences at the sound of his mystery-shrouded name and of how governments fell as he stepped out of faraway capitals."

To Rita herself he was also a shadowy gentleman – a well-meaning but remote parent who saw to it that she would be educated by English governesses and private tutors, that she would be presented at Court, and that she would accept an arranged marriage to the most eligible of her Armenian cousins. As it turned out, that marriage, not always temperamentally compatible, was amicable from the beginning and soon became loving. In her early forties, the death of her illustrious father allowed Rita to assess a life she had come to regard as one long submission to a kind of genteel house arrest. With a decisiveness of which she had never before been capable, she turned her back on all that she was entitled to in England, moved to Paris, arranged a mutually agreeable separation from her husband, and resolved to spend the rest of her life exploring, to view at first hand every example of the creative impulse from the time of the cave paintings of Lascaux, then to comprehend the variety and vitality of lives lived beyond the cocoonlike existence to which she had long been committed. Charged with curiosity and sustained by wonder, she remains the most purely motivated traveler I have ever met, partly because – beneath the trappings of a kind of oriental haute couture – she was still a little girl in a pinafore and Mary Janes on her way to a party that never ended, simply because it never quite took place.

But before she was able to act on her new intentions came World War II, during which she joined the forces of the French underground – the maquis – with the particular assignment of rescuing, then finding hiding places for, British pilots who'd been shot down.

We first met when, by the luck of the draw, we'd found ourselves seated side by side in an open boat taking us to the island of Skyros and the graveside of Rupert Brooke, whose poetry, I was delighted to learn, she considered as high-toned phony and meretricious as I did. I soon learned that she had been everywhere – twice. Long years before China was opened to the West, she had been to China – twice. Traveling alone for most of every year, she would book passage on one or the other of small ships carrying art historians, archaeologists, or botanists to obscure destinations from Antarctica to Iceland, sometimes choosing itineraries back to back or three or four in a row.

Over a period of ten years or so, whenever I dared or could afford to, I'd leave my classroom to join her at some distant dock or airport – reunions that inevitably began in tears of unabashed sentiment, as though we were principals in still another recognition scene, and ended in the confidence that this would go on forever. Even to ourselves, we were a most unlikely couple. To me, she was the empress Zenobia, fleeing on a long-necked camel – not from jeopardy, but into freedom. In her eyes, I was "a prosperous Boston schoolboy with a bookbag and a blazer." For all that, we dwelt in wonder, accepting what we saw without the need to speak of what we felt and, for all of our differences, looking out the same window.

On January 4, 1976, it was my treat to show her Jacmel, a ghost town, once coffee-rich, left over from the nineteenth century's Age of Iron and now preserved in a thin layer of dust. Located on the southern coast of Haiti, Jacmel was then accessible only by sea or by helicopter. I had been there once before – and so, with the authority of a one-eyed man in the kingdom of the blind, I led Rita through its silent streets, desiccated gardens, and barren marketplaces until, a little grimy with funereal dust, we came to the one ramshackle hotel where we might get a Coke and a sandwich. As we sat down at a table laid with oilcloth and artificial flowers, I was intrigued to note the presence of four or five men in dark suits seated at the only other occupied table. Unless my eyes deceived me, among them was André Malraux, then Charles de Gaulle's minister of culture and a hero of my youth for his landmark novels *Man's Fate* and *Man's*

Hope. "Don't look now," I said, "but do I see what I think I see?" Incapable of a furtive glance, Rita turned her head. But only for a split second as, on their feet and clashing like gladiators, she and Malraux embraced in a storm of French expostulation.

Forty-eight hours later, in fulfillment of an old promise, I brought her to Key West and ensconced her in the laid-back ambience (some would call it benign neglect) of David Wolkowsky's Pier House. Leaving her to explorations she liked to make on foot, next day I hid out in raffish bars I hoped she'd never find, down streets with busted sidewalks I hoped she'd never tread. What would she make of a town at the end of the line that reveled in squalor, cultivated waywardness, and, calling itself Conch Republic, regarded Florida as an enemy country somewhere toward the north? When I joined her that evening she was wearing sandals and a ponderous necklace of shells and I was in for a lecture. "Why did you wait so long to bring me to this place," she said. "I love it even more than Hong Kong!"

Barely one year later, Rita accepted the judgment of her physicians that her heart could no longer withstand the demands of travel. But she could not accept advice to the effect that henceforth her days would be spent in the effortless domesticity a staff of servants would provide. True to her word, she retrieved a vial of some instantly lethal substance which, along with her maquis colleagues, she had been given in the event of Nazi torture. On Easter Sunday she dined with the family she had summoned to Paris and the friends she had enlisted to entertain them. As I learned from one of them, it was the merriest and most carefree of occasions – in the midst of which Rita excused herself and retired to a room from which she would never emerge.

Travel as diversion; travel as a means. In pursuit of one I would submit to the seductions of the other – but not until the lessons I had learned made the distinction negligible. I've had my moments, as the old song says – and, by your leave, I'll conclude this self-indulgent discourse on a note of nostalgia for one more of them.

September 25, 1967. The *Queen Elizabeth,* largest ship in the world, twenty-seven years old, is bound westward; at some point in the early morning she will meet and pass the *Queen Mary,* the next-largest ship in the world, thirty-one years old, bound east. This will be their final meeting, their last sight of each other, ever. For more than two decades they have been the proudest sisters on the ocean, deferential to each other, secure in the knowledge that they are the most celebrated things on water since rafts went floating down the Tigris and Euphrates.

Notices of this encounter have been broadcast and posted throughout the ship. But as usual at this hour (12:10 A.M.) most passengers have gone to bed, leaving only a few individuals strolling and dawdling on the promenade deck. Most of these have chosen to be alone; and they are a bit sheepish, a bit embarrassed, as though ashamed to be seen in the thrall of sentiment, even by others equally enthralled.

As the appointed moment draws near, they begin to disappear from the promenade deck, only to reappear in the darkness of the broad glassed-in observation area on boat deck forward. They stand apart from one another and do not speak, their eyes fixed on the visible horizon to the west as the vibration of the ship gives a slightly stroboscopic blur to everything they see. The mid-Atlantic sky is windless, a dome of hard stars; the ocean glows, an immense conjunction of inseparable water and air. Entranced, the late watchers try to pick out some dot of light that will not turn out to be a star. Hushed, the minutes pass. These ten or twelve of the faithful in their shadowy stances might be postulants on a Vermont hillside, waiting in their gowns for the end of the world. Then the light of certainty. Almost as is if she were climbing the watery slopes of the globe, the oncoming *Queen* shows one wink at her topmost mast, then two.

Spotted, she grows quickly in size and brightness. In the dim silence of the enclosure there are mutters, the click of binoculars against plate glass, an almost reverential sense of breath withheld. On she comes, the *Mary*, with a swiftness that takes everyone by surprise: together the great ships, more than 160,000 tons of steel, are closing the gap that separates them at a speed of nearly sixty miles an hour. Cutting the water deeply, pushing it aside in great crested arrowheads, they veer toward one another almost as if to embrace, and all the lights blaze out, scattering the dark. The huge funnels glow in their Cunard red, the basso-profundo horns belt out a sound that has the quality less of a salute than of one long mortal cry. Standing at attention on the starboard wing of his flying bridge, the *Elizabeth*'s captain doffs his hat; on the starboard wing of the *Mary*, her captain does the same.

As though they had not walked and climbed there but had been somehow instantly transported to the topmost deck, the few passengers who have watched the *Mary* come out of the night now watch her go. All through the episode, mere minutes long, have come giggles and petulant whispers from sequestered corners of the top deck. Indifferent to the moment, untouched by the claims of history, youngsters not yet born when the two *Queens* were the newest wonders of the world cling together in adolescent parodies of passion and do not bother even to look up. As the darkness closes over and the long wakes are joined, the sentimentalists stand for a while watching the ocean recover its seamless immensity. Then, one by one, like people dispersing downhill after a burial, they find their way to their cabins and close their doors.

RUTH WHITMAN

The Journey of a Jewish-American Poet

[DORTORT WRITERS' INSTITUTE]

Born into a loquacious, tempestuous second-generation Russian-Jewish family in the early 1920s, I remember – an early memory – my grandfather holding me on his lap and singing Russian and Yiddish lullabies in his deep baritone. That music, that *nigun*, was to stay in my head, disappear, and resurface again in my forties. In the 1920s, however, when Yiddish poetry and theater were flourishing on New York's Lower East Side, my grandfather was a friend of many poets and actors. When I was six he took me to the Café Brevoort on Fifth Avenue to show me off to some of his cronies.

But as I grew up I wanted to shun what I regarded as the ghetto mentality – the overprotectiveness of my parents, their narrow shtetl view of the world. I was determined to escape. At nineteen I seized my opportunity. A sophomore at New York University, I was encouraged by my English professor to apply for a scholarship to the Bread Loaf School of English in Middlebury, Vermont.

There I discovered a new world – the world I had been yearning for. It was the summer of 1941, just before the United States entered the Second World War, but there was still a kind of *dolce far niente* mood up on the Vermont mountain. The king of the mountain was of course Robert Frost, who was talking about the necessity of writing an American epic about the Civil War. The idea of writing a long narrative poem was then planted in me, to be attempted much later. I studied with John Crowe Ransom, the philosopher Theodore Meyer Greene, and drank beer with

Theodore Roethke, whose first book of poems had just come out. Cedric Whitman, the young Robert Frost poet from Harvard, whose book was being printed at Bread Loaf, invited me to come and live with him in Cambridge.

We eloped six weeks later, with the encouragement of Louis Untermeyer, and to the consternation of my parents. My father threatened to sit shivah for me as though I were dead, but my mother forgave us. I felt triumphant. But it was not to last. I applied to Radcliffe College and was told that the registrar would waive the Jewish quota only because I was marrying a gentile Harvard student. Cambridge just before the Second World War was strongly anti-Semitic, and my new husband advised me not to tell his friends that I was Jewish. That stung me. It began a long experience of shaken identity—as a woman, as a poet, and as a Jew. All three conditions made me in some sense a pariah in that society.

During the time of the European Holocaust, the war against the Jews, I had to ask myself if I would be willing to identify myself as a Jew. I found that the answer was yes, despite the horror, yes. Three children and two husbands later, I married my third husband, a passionate secular Jew, a painter, who gave added incentive to my wish to accept my history.

I began to think in Jewish metaphor. My second book, *The Marriage Wig*, based its images and argument on the medieval custom of shaving the bride's head in order to make her acceptable to her husband. She was then compelled to wear a *sheitel*, or marriage wig.

THE MARRIAGE WIG

If you're going to marry, make sure you first
know whom you're going to divorce.
                                        —Yiddish Proverb

1.
The Mishnah says I blind you with my hair
that when I bind it in a net
my fingers waylay my friends:
that in a close house I shake loose
the Pleiades into your kitchen.

How can I let you see me, past and future,
blemishes and dust? Must I
shear away my hair and wear
the wig the wisemen say? Will you

receive me, rejoice me, take me for your wall?

To any man not blind, a wig is false. . . .

Needing to examine the role of the married woman, especially the Jewish woman, I wrote a series of poems on cutting a woman's hair.

CUTTING THE JEWISH BRIDE'S HAIR

It's to possess more than the skin
that those old world Jews
exacted the hair of their brides.
        Good husband, lover of the Torah,
        does the calligraphy of your bride's hair
        interrupt your page?

Before the clownish friction of flesh
creating out of nothing
a mockup of its begetters,
a miraculous puppet of God,
you must first divorce her from her vanity.

She will snip off her pride,
cut back her appetite to be devoured,
she will keep herself well braided,
her love's furniture will not endanger you,
        but this little amputation
        will shift the balance of the universe.

After this book I began to think of writing about the lives of other women. I was dissatisfied with the limitations of the short lyric as well as the limitations of writing about the experience of a white middle-class woman living in comparative luxury and safety. I wanted to move out of my own experience and into someone else's life, to know how other women in other times and places had reacted to repression, danger, loss, and mortality. I wanted to write in the voices of real women whose lives had the potential of being mythologized, especially a woman during the Holocaust, although I knew I wasn't quite ready.

I had already written in the voice of Lizzie Borden, with whose frustration and rage I identified in the years of my earlier marriages. But now, in the 1970s, I was concerned with issues of survival.

Tamsen Donner appeared to me when I was coming out of ether after a minor operation. Half asleep, I discovered I was writing a passage on the lined yellow pad I always keep beside my bed. I was on the third page, writing a poem not in my own voice or era. I seemed to be a pioneer woman in the nineteenth century who was coming to a last range of mountains, wondering if I could get across safely with my family. I began to read women's journals, accounts of early pioneer journeys, and recognized Tamsen Donner in George Stewart's *Ordeal by Hunger*, which I had read in 1938 as a girl of sixteen. She had been born on the coast of Massachusetts, was a poet and teacher, had two families and an adventurous spirit. She felt familiar to me.

With a grant from the National Endowment, I traveled together with my eighty-year-old father and fifteen-year-old son along the California trail, following Tamsen Donner's footsteps and keeping a journal, as she had done. I thought of the journey in its literal sense as a typical American experience, moving from innocence to disaster; as one heroic woman's history, moving from dependence to courageous selfhood; and as a parallel to the experience of the Holocaust, when Jews were called upon to cope with and survive horrendous loss and annihilation.

APRIL 10, 1847, BY ALDER CREEK.

How can I store against coming loss?
What faculties of the heart
can I bring against this parting?

We traveled across the land
towards winter not towards spring

I watched the children become solemn and thin
our wagons and housewares
brittle
              depleted

When I buried my boxes
my watercolors and oils my writing desk

I felt I had given all I could part with.

Finally, having lost everyone, Tamsen Donner writes:

WHERE IS THE WEST

If my boundary stops here
I have daughters to draw new maps on the world
they will draw the lines of my face
they will draw with my gestures my voice
they will speak my words thinking they have invented them
they will invent them
they will invent me
I will be planted again and again
I will wake in the eyes of their children's children
they will speak my words

The triumph of survival, despite death and annihilation, was brought home to me in 1974, when I first visited Israel as a guest of the Israeli government. It was after the Yom Kippur War, when the euphoria at having established a new Jewish state received its first blow. I fell in love with that tiny, courageous country, and knew I was moving toward a work that would express my new perceptions.

MARIA OLT

On a hillside in Jerusalem
under the hammer sun, she lifts

a little carob tree, the tree of John
the Baptist, and sets it

into its hole. Solid as a house,
she is called Righteous, a Christian

who hid Jews in Hungary. Her hair clings
around her broad face as she bends

with the hoe, carefully heaping the soil
around the roots. She builds a rim of dirt

on the downhill side and pours water from
the heavy bucket. She waits until the earth

sucks the water up, then pours again
with a slow wrist. The workmen

sent to help her, stand aside, helpless.
She straightens up. Her eyes are wet.

Tears come to her easily.
The small Jewish woman she saved

stands beside her, dryeyed.
Thirtyfive years ago, as they watched

the death train pass, faces and hands
silent between the slats, the girl

had cried, I want to go with them!
No, said Maria, you must understand,

if you go, I will go with you.

I knew it was now time for me to write a narrative about a heroic
woman in the Second World War. I had long known the diary and letters
of Hanna Senesh, but it came as a sudden inspiration that here was my
Jewish woman, an Israeli heroine who was part of the rescue mission from

Palestine to Hungary in 1944, the year I graduated from Radcliffe College.

We were enough alike for me to begin to enter her life. She was a year older than me, had been brought up in an assimilated household, and came late to her sense of identity as a Jew. We both wrote poetry from early childhood, played the piano, led a life that seemed to be secure. When she saw that a literary or academic life would be impossible for her in Hungary under Nazi rule, she emigrated to Palestine in 1939, just as the Second World War began. She worked on Kibbutz Sdot Yam on the Mediterranean, learning to be a farmer. As news spread of the Nazi death camps, she determined to go back to Hungary to help rescue the remaining Jews and also to help her mother, who had remained in Budapest. When the British finally allowed her to set off on her parachute rescue mission in 1944, it was too late. The Germans had already invaded and occupied Hungary. But Hanna was determined to walk from Yugoslavia, where she had been forced to land, to Budapest. As soon as she crossed the border, the Gestapo arrested her.

I made several trips to Israel to interview Hanna's mother and brother, who had both managed to survive, and to meet two of the parachutists who had flown with Hanna. I visited her kibbutz and her grave, and steeped myself in as much material about the history of the war as I could find. The reading alone was a shaking experience, but I told myself that if these heroic people could live through those terrible days, I could at least endure reading about them.

BUDAPEST: JUNE 1944

They've been beating me for three days. . . .

After the first shock
it's like letting a wave of flame singe your hand:
first a sharp sensation, then no feeling.
I watch myself like a person in a dream
while they invent devices to break me down.

But I never scream.
Screaming means it's happening to me.
I step back and watch it happen around me . . .

                    I say
no   no   to myself
don't let them have a sign that I feel it:

think of the blue-green sea that I saw every night
from my tent under the old stars,
the cool winds of evening:

think of that hill in Jerusalem,
the little lights shining in the villages,
breathe the aromatic Judaean air,
watch the sun set in the Old City,
the shadows creeping up the towers,
pulling the bruised light behind them:

you see: I feel nothing.

It is only my body flopping like a fish.

It is only my body that bleeds.

And then, in November 1944, when the Russians and Allies were closing
in on Budapest, the Nazis took Hanna out of prison and shot her.

I'm standing in the ancient ruins at Caesarea
among the shattered Roman columns
lying in seawater
and I see
the broken statue of a woman
missing entirely above the waist:

but I can tell
from the white hand
lifting the folds of her garment,
from her hard thigh
beneath the fluted skirt,
from the sure grace of her bent knee
and the foot she is leaning on
in its imaginary sandal
the foot taking her weight

I can tell
she is there

inside the broken body
she is complete.

Since the early 1960s, at the same time that I was writing my own poetry, I had been translating modern Yiddish poetry. I could hear my
grandfather's *nigun* again. Impelled by a great curiosity about Yiddish poetry, I had started studying Yiddish on my own, and then took a course at
Harvard Hillel in elementary Yiddish. I was partly motivated by a sarcas-
tic article written by Isaac Bashevis Singer about a dinner given by the
Poetry Society of America where I received a prize for one of my poems.
He lamented that this "oriental-looking poet with a *goyishe* [non-Jewish]
name" didn't know a word of her heritage.

When I reached a reading knowledge of Yiddish, using a dictionary, I
visited Singer and asked him what I should do to learn about Yiddish poetry. He said, "Translate me. I need a poet." For two years I translated
some of his stories – an education in itself – and then he declared me
ready to make an anthology of modern Yiddish poetry. It was published
in 1966 by David Way, the publisher of my first book of lyrics. Way sin-
gled out Jacob Glatstein as the most remarkable of the fourteen poets in
my anthology and asked me to translate an entire volume of his work.

With a Bunting Institute Fellowship in poetry, I began a five-year association with one of the most powerful and original of contemporary Yiddish poets. His acerbic language about Jewish life and twentieth-century
issues, his bold linguistic inventions, his daring free verse and Whit-
manesque lines helped to free my own rather limited lyric style. He died
in 1972, just before *The Selected Poems of Jacob Glatstein* was published.

MOZART

I dreamed that
the gentiles crucified Mozart
and buried him in a pauper's grave.
But the Jews made him a man of God
and blessed his memory.

I, his apostle, ran all over the world,
converting everyone I met,
and wherever I caught a Christian
I made him a Mozartian.

How wonderful is the musical testament
of this divine man!
How nailed through with song
his shining hands!
In his greatest need
all the fingers of this crucified
singer were laughing.
And in his most crying grief
he loved his neighbor's ear
more than himself.

How poor and stingy —
compared with Mozart's legacy
is the Sermon on the Mount.

— Jacob Glatstein

Abraham Sutzkever, the other giant of modern Yiddish poetry, was the first Yiddish poet I translated for my anthology, and I always felt a special obligation to translate more of his work. Of the fourteen poets I had originally translated, he is the only one still living. When I was in Jerusalem in 1985 on a Fulbright writer-in-residence fellowship, I went to see him. I asked him what book he would like me to translate. He asked me to work on *The Fiddle Rose*, a deeply metaphysical book of poems about the resurrection of creativity after the Holocaust. The book was published in 1990, and Sutzkever, now old and infirm, came to the United States to read with me at the 92nd Street YMHA Poetry Center in New York.

Preparing a third, enlarged edition of *An Anthology of Modern Yiddish Poetry*, I lately return to some of Sutzkever's earlier lyrics:

POETRY

The last dark violet
plum on the tree,
delicate and tender as the pupil of an eye,
blots out in the dewy night
all love, visions, trembling,
and at the morningstar the dew
becomes airier—
that's poetry. Touch it without
letting it show the print of your fingers.

—Abraham Sutzkever

As I become older, my personal poems turn more and more to the
people and events of my early years, an experience that is common to
writers of every generation. Here is the title poem of my most recent collection, poems selected from 1963 to 1990:

LAUGHING GAS

It was near the Coliseum, RKO,
in the Bronx,
on a broad street lined with trees
where the dentist, an old sweetheart
of my mother's, gave me gas
for a six-year-old molar.

I laughed.

            I swam inside
bubbles of laughter
in a leather-smelling office,
while my tooth floated away.

Then out on the street,
on the trolley,
all the way home and through the night,
I vomited.

I vomited my lost babyhood,
separations to come,
the plane over Reno, buses and trains
pulling out, each future diminution:
hair, teeth, breath.

My grandmother said:
laugh before breakfast,
cry before dinner.

And the final poem of that book:

IN A MIRROR

Sometimes I can see the old woman
in the child, the child in the woman,
a game I play, traveling
in a plane or train, imagining
the businessman next to me a toddler
in diapers, or that mischievous redheaded
infant a woman of forty.

My ages, stacked behind me, blow past
like cards in a hurricane:
the blackeyed four-year-old
with a ball in her dimpled fist;
the fourteen-year-old bathing beauty
with barely defined curves.

But who is this woman in my mirror?
Who is this interloper?
Looking more closely, I recognize
the dark eyes and the high cheekbones,
echoing those ancestors
ravished by the Mongols on the Russian
steppes. In the end it's the bones
that tell who you have been.

KIMBERLY M. BLAESER

Entering the Canon: Our Place in World Literature

[RETURNING THE GIFT: A FESTIVAL
OF NORTH AMERICAN NATIVE WRITERS]

I want to share with you some of the important things I have heard people say about the place of Native peoples in the canon of world literature. Simon Ortiz says, "Our identity and our image is inter-American." Leslie Silko says we have to "disregard those boundaries that have been drawn by the illegal United States government." Gloria Bird addresses the way that colonization shows up in criticism in the notions of "the center and the margin." Mike Wilson looks at the different aesthetic of Native American literature and comments that (in classes on Native literature) it is rather strange to ask for an analytical essay on a form that attempts to undercut the analytical structure or tradition. Carter Revard talks about the action he has taken in including Native American literature in the canon: in his Great Western Works in Translation course he teaches the Navajo creation story. So the work has begun; but there is a long way yet to go.

In 1991 *Poetry East* put out an issue featuring Native American poetry. It was a good issue and I was enjoying it immensely until I took a look at the contributors' notes. It had been divided into "Native Americans" and "The Poets" – as if the Native American contributors were not also poets. If the editors wanted to accord special distinction to the Indigenous writers, why did they not use the title "Native American Poets"? These designations troubled me a great deal. I sent a letter to one of the issue editors explaining my objection, but darned if it mustn't have gotten lost in the mail because it was never answered. So I wrote this poem:

"NATIVE AMERICANS" VS. "THE POETS"
(SOME THOUGHTS I HAD WHILE READING
POETRY EAST)

You know that solitary Indian
sitting in his fringed leathers
on his horse at the rise of the hill
face painted, holding a lance
there just at the horizon?
That guy's got a Ph.D.
He's *the* Indian for Mankato State or Carroll College

Indian professors at universities throughout the country
Exhibit A,
No B, no C, just solitary romanticized A
Not much of a threat that way

Real trouble is
America
still doesn't know what to do with Indians

Looked for your books lately in Powell's
or 57th St. Books?
Check first in folklore or anthropology
Found Louis' *Wolfsong* in black literature
Hell no wonder we all got an identity crisis

You a poet?
No, I just write Indian stuff

Clearly the mentality that makes a distinction between Native Americans who are poets and "real" writers, between Native Americans who teach at universities and "real" professors, is to be resisted. However, the manifestations of this mentality are often very subtle. The intellectual elitism that perpetuates racism and classism asserts that American history begins with European invasion, that oral history is "prehistory," that oral tradition or oral literature is inferior to written tradition and written literature, and that American Indian studies in general have adjunct status.

For two weeks at the end of June 1992 I was in Pembroke, North Carolina, participating in a summer institute for high school teachers. The institute centered on Native American literature, history, and culture, with the idea that the teachers would gain a greater understanding of Native American studies and be able to incorporate ideas and material into their curriculum. On the first day, as the teachers introduced themselves, several of them linked their attendance to gaining materials to use during American Indian Week. I was getting twitchy hearing this, you know – but I was good. (I'm telling this story because it's not too often that I get to tell about my good behavior.) Anyway, I restrained myself and decided to bide my time. Well, as luck would have it, before too many days had passed one of the participants challenged the idea of having *an* American Indian week as if Indians didn't belong in the other fifty-one weeks of the year, as if they didn't fit into the study of history, literature, philosophy, and so on. Then at the closing session one of the participants commented (as if responding to my silent first-day question – maybe I wasn't so cool after all) that she came in thinking about just getting through Indian week because she didn't feel she knew enough to do anything more. She said she used to grab a film or an audiotape or a lesson plan like a lifeline just to fill the time, but that now, knowing more, she was ready to do more.

The battle for inclusion in the canon of world literature has to do with more than having your writing sandwiched between Norman Mailer and Joan Didion in some publisher's collection. If Indian literature is not included in the canon of American letters, if it is not read and studied in our colleges as legitimate literature, then Native peoples remain invisible in society, and the teaching in our grade schools and high schools will not improve.

Just making requirements, however, does not seem to me to be the answer. Having a cultural diversity requirement does not mean good material will be taught. Indeed, ill-informed teachers, perhaps with the best intentions, may simply perpetuate stereotypes. So we don't want a niche, a token week or class separated from the rest of the curriculum. We don't want mere inclusion and we don't want marginal status. Instead we want quality attention, we want the influences of tribal literature on the general categories of American literature and world literature recognized.

The distinctions that have been made regarding the style, method, themes, and plots of Indigenous writing are, for the most part, legitimate. Native Americans have a distinct and important voice in American letters, a voice that speaks about what William Bevis calls "homing in" (in contrast to the "wandering" in American literature that Lance Henson mentions), a voice that speaks about natural cycles, spiritual connections, family, community, and place. We are not content, however, with the kind of attention that merely says the writing by Indian people is unique in this or that way. There are connections between tribal literatures and the work of major American and world authors. There are connections between tribal literatures of the United States and Canada and Mexico and South America that disregard geographical boundaries. Indeed, scholars are beginning to recognize that Native American literature has a great deal in common with other postcolonial literatures throughout the world.

A theory of Valentin Volosinov helps illuminate the place and significance of Native American literature, and draws connections among the work of Native peoples throughout the world. James Zebroski says that for Volosinov writing style itself "evokes and can help reproduce existing social-class relations." In *Marxism and the Philosophy of Language*, Volosinov (or Mikhail Bakhtin; there is an identity problem here) postulates two basic styles of writing: the monologic or linear, associated with the ruling classes; and the dialogic or pictorial, associated with the under- or working classes. The first, the linear or monologic, Zebroski characterizes as one that "draws hard, clearly demarcated boundaries" and "tends to move toward purity and unity." The second, the pictorial or dialogic, is "a mixture of popular and unofficial genres, full of the voices of other people"; it "infiltrates boundaries and blurs established genres," and "tends to mix texts and their authority." The second, of course, quite accurately describes the characteristic style of Native American writing: "a mixture of popular and unofficial genres, full of the voices of other people" – think of Leslie Marmon Silko's *Storyteller*, a mixture of family stories and remembrances, conversations, photos, as well as poetry and fiction, full of the voices of Aunt Susie, Grandpa Hank, Aunt Alice, Simon Ortiz, and Nora; "infiltrates boundaries and blurs established genres" – think of Momaday's blurring of the boundaries of the personal, the mythic, and the historic in *The Way to Rainy Mountain;* and "tends to mix texts and their authority" – think of any number of Native American writers who intertwine traditional myth with present-day story, who employ myth as the truth necessary to understand the present; think of those who give authority to the voices of animals and other beings. So stylistically we can see Native American writing as a part of this larger body of literature of the so-called underclasses, a part of the dialogic style of writing.

But perhaps more important to note is intention and purpose. Writing in a dialogic style can be a conscious challenge to the monologic style, which endorses the existing social and political system, and thus a symbolic challenge to that very system. Put more simply, we can write a revolution. Filling our writing with the many voices from our tribal communities and families, according them status, is one way of attempting to work for the continuance of family and community. Filling our writing with ceremony and song is more than a mere recording and it is more than pretty literature. It becomes an act of survival.

Let me give you an example of writing as revolution, using Linda Hogan's poem "Workaday" from *Savings*. In "Workaday," Hogan writes: "Now I go to the University / and out for lunch / and listen to the higher-ups / tell me all they have read / about Indians / and how to analyze this poem." It seems to me that much is going on here. Hogan recognizes and exposes the colonization of identity and the colonization of literature; she exposes subtle racism and the subtle moves employed to preserve the established power system. Here the racism is manifested in appropriation of identity: "tell me all they have read about Indians"; and the move to preserve power is manifested in the arrogant presumption of superior understanding: "tell me . . . how to analyze this poem." Intellectual elitism is manifested in the poem when the "higher-ups" assume the position of ultimate explicator. The racism lies, not in the claim to understand the identity and literature of another, but in the claim to understand it *better* than the spokesperson. But Hogan's poem itself becomes a revolutionary act, an act of resistance. With "Workaday" she both exposes and opposes the attempt at literary colonization. Hogan and other writers will not allow Indian literature to be patronized.

There are many more issues that seem important in a discussion of the place of Indigenous writing in the canon of American and world literatures: What makes writing Native American? The author's identity (a

BIA enrollment card)? The subject of the work? Or the style and approach of the writing? Since cultural values are clearly embodied in a people's literature, since different cultures have different aesthetic values, by whose standards should Native people's writing be evaluated — that of another culture, or that of their own? Is there a danger that inclusion in the canon can work to advance the designs of assimilation, and how do we prevent our artistic and cultural identities from being manhandled and subsumed in the established system? These are some of the questions we need to think about and talk about.

Look around: we clearly are a force to be reckoned with, we have a literary identity, we have a place in world literature, recognized or unrecognized by the intellectual elite. May our place always be one of survival, of continuance, and of revolution.

M. NOURBESE PHILIP

A Piece of Land Surrounded

[POETRY SOCIETY OF AMERICA: CARIBBEAN POETRY FESTIVAL]

> . . . remember the future
> Imagine the past
> See the present and deal with it. It is a
> part of history.
> — Carlos Fuentes

I have lost my place, or my place has deserted me. This may be the dilemma of the West Indian writer abroad: that he hungers for nourishment from a soil which he (as an ordinary citizen) could not at present endure. The pleasure and the paradox of my own exile is that I belong wherever I am. My role, it seems, has rather to do with time and change than with the geography of circumstances; and yet there is always an acre of ground in the New World which keeps growing echoes in my head.

> — George Lamming, *The Pleasures of Exile*

We began by being a European idea. We cannot be understood if it's forgotten that we are a chapter in the history of European utopias. It is enough to recall that Europe is the fruit – in some ways involuntary – of European history, whereas we are its premeditated creation. . . . As soon as he reached our shores the European immigrant was changed into a projectile aimed at the future.

> — Octavio Paz, *A Literature of Foundations*

A piece of land surrounded by water – an island – one island – a Caribbean island – a definition eluding definition – land surrounded by water, by a history of interruptions, or silence; an island – not merely land *and* water, but land *surrounded* by water. That powerful mediating factor in island life, water, separation by water, an isolation that makes fighting over islands, initially by colonial powers for sugar, and more recently by superpowers for their minds – think of Cuba, Grenada – so easy.

What if we played with the definition? An island: a piece of land *floating*, not merely surrounded, in water. The shift, ever so slight, of emphasis so that the isolation and separation implicit in "surrounded" is diminished; in its floating, which is not passive but requires a state of relaxed awareness in which the surrounding sea bears the weight, the island assumes more autonomy.

Let us, however, remain with the original definition, since it is entirely the most appropriate place to begin an essay, in both senses, into the understanding of the Caribbean – islands surrounded. By the sea and by the colonial condition that continues to beset them. It *is* the most appropriate place to start, since with less than twenty-four hours' notice the minister of works for Trinidad and Tobago recently (1992) announced a 60 percent increase in airfares between Trinidad and Tobago, bringing to the surface all the latent and not-so-latent tensions that have existed between these two islands ever since their union in 1899.

Succinctly put, the source of the tension is that Tobagonians *need* to go to Trinidad for most essential services; the reverse is not true for Trinidadians. The equality and identicalness explicit in the word "twin," as in "twin island state," becomes a mockery when the *need* for communication generated by being a "piece of land surrounded by water" is further exacerbated and fraught by the necessity of experiencing the outer world through an/other piece of land, itself surrounded by water. Any attempt to understand the piece of land that is Tobago must start here: Trinidad is the lens through which Tobago is seen, or as is so often the case, not seen, and through which Tobago sees the surrounding world.

The timing of this piece is fortuitous on account of a decision in July 1992, by Justice Clebert Brooks, on a habeas corpus application brought on behalf of the Muslimeen (Black Muslim) leader Abu Bakr and his supporters, which held that they were all being detained illegally.

On July 27, 1990, Abu Bakr and his supporters stormed the Houses of Parliament, which resulted in the death and wounding of many people, as well as enormous damage to Port of Spain [in Trinidad]. After a six-day standoff between the Muslimeen and the army, the former surrendered into the custody of the government and its armed forces.* Lawyers for the Muslimeen argued that President Carter had granted them an amnesty during his term of office. Almost two years later to the day, Justice Brooks would decide that, pursuant to the Constitution, the amnesty *was* valid, that the Muslimeen were to be released – though not immediately – and that they were entitled to monetary compensation; this despite the fact that at the time the president signed the said amnesty, members of Parliament were lying hog-tied and wounded.

The decision is significant for many reasons, not the least of which is what it says about how shallow the roots of independence grow in these islands; it is a decision that emphasizes how little the connection is between the law and the people, and fails to acknowledge the vital connection between a lived jurisprudence and the law. We ought not to be surprised, however, if we understand the nature of law in colonial societies. It is, I believe, a decision that will have untold repercussions, both for this society and for the wider Caribbean.

In 1991, an exile returned, I began a year's residence on a particular piece of land surrounded by water – Tobago, where I was born and spent my early years. Ostensibly, I was here to complete a novel, the germ of which had begun ten years earlier – also in Tobago. It often happens to a writer engaged on a particular story or poem that another one is being written, below the surface – the sea of one story floating the other. The challenge then becomes how to withdraw in order to allow what has to be written to emerge. For me, the "story" that wanted out, wanted to tell itself, is one of islandness and its transformation into *I-landness*. And colonialism. It seemed the island, this particular island – a piece of land – *I-land* surrounded by – was trying to shape through writing my understanding of it, and so of the Caribbean. The very process of forming an island would replicate itself, as if understanding – my understanding – had been surrounded and submerged in a great sea of knowledge and history – European, primarily – and through the process of writing *I-land*

*Lawyers for the Muslimeen immediately launched legal challenges, by means of a habeas corpus application, to the incarceration on the grounds that there had been an amnesty. When the Trinidad courts rejected the habeas corpus application, Muslimeen lawyers appealed to the privy council, which ordered the local courts to deal with the matter of amnesty and the habeas corpus application.

would surface, become visible. And float. Not merely or only surrounded by, but balancing itself, as one must do in floating, understanding the surrounding waters, its dangers, using its strengths.

Traditionally, the writings shaping and surrounding these islands have come from those who first captured them and fought over them, erasing not only the ligaments binding the first peoples to the land but also the contributions of those laboring to bring them into production – the African and the Asian. Silence and words – European words – would, in fact, be the mechanism shaping these islands, contouring them into separateness, except where cultural retentions such as orality and music and dance helped them to float in the sea of Europeanness. Essentially, each would remain "a piece of land surrounded by water" – an island, a people isolated, surrounded by empty legalisms emptied of any relevance to their reality – a piece of land – a people – surrounded by –

Writing is not what the majority of the people in these islands turn to for the information that matters to them, or for their understanding of themselves. They, like the islands they inhabit, have been surrounded by writing and writings ever since the European began his formulation of them, and they know too well how little writing has served their best interests.

Five hundred years ago Cristóbal Colón came upon Watling Island: he enc(o)untered another world and that first enc(o)unter with the land and the Natives would be the palimpsest for Europe's subsequent enc(o)unter with the New World. The New World would become both womb *(cunt)* and wound *(cut)*. So, too, my encounter and engagement with this island – *I-land* – of birth, Tobago, would, in turn, become a microcosm of my engagement with the larger issues of exile and displacement, identity, racism and colonialism. All of the issues around that original exile – from Africa – would find resonances in my enc(o)unter with Tobago. Tobago would become a surrogate Africa – "a piece of land surrounded by" water and History and histories and memories and re-memberings. . . .

Two books shaped time in the Caribbean for me, the returning native: *The Pleasures of Exile* (1960) by George Lamming, and *A Morning at the Office* (1950) by Edgar Mittelholzer. I would read the former for the first time, the latter for the second, both within the first few weeks of being "back in the Caribbean," often facing the Caribbean sea, watching and hearing the surf pound the coast – "a piece of land surrounded by" – being eroded by – water. Mittelholzer's brilliant study of class, caste, and racial interactions in Trinidad underscored the long-forgotten reasons for my fleeing Trinidad twenty-four years ago for the more racially polarized but strangely less complicated society of white North America: If you weren't in you were out, and if you were black, brown, or yellow, coffee, café au lait, or whatever, you weren't in.

For the Caribbean writer, the impulse and pressure to exile that Lamming described was still very much alive; the forces propelling Caribbean writers to refuse the separation of "surrounded by," which is not only a physical separation, are as relevant today as they were when Lamming first wrote his book. Today the terrain is not so much unfriendly as indifferent to writing, just as it was when he and others of his generation left the Caribbean. Maybe the people distrust what writing – the surrounding sea of colonial and European writing – has done to them, trusting more in their orality.

The backdrop to both these books was *The Tempest*, which Lamming deals with extensively and brilliantly in *Pleasures* and which I kept on my desk, occasionally reading odd bits. For many Caribbean writers *The Tempest* presents a paradigm for colonial society, while the relationship between Prospero and Caliban has been a blueprint for the problematic that language presents for colonial peoples who trace their linguistic genealogy back to Caliban, betrayed by Prospero. The white European gives Caliban, the black man, language. But before that, Caliban had himself given generously – in the way the peoples of the Caribbean, the Americas, Asia, and Africa have always behaved toward the European – of himself and his island, his piece of land surrounded.

Miranda, the white woman, also teaches Caliban: "I pitied thee, / Took pains to make thee speak, taught thee each hour / One thing or other." There's also Ariel, sometimes seen as the bureaucrat – the "half breed." But what of the black woman? We hear of Sycorax, Caliban's mother, the "blue-ey'd hag," the "damn'd witch" who, Shakespeare tells us, lay with "the devil himself," and produced Caliban the black man. Was Sycorax a black woman, perhaps? Argier, from which she came, lay somewhere in the Mediterranean, which connects northern Africa with southern Europe.

Sycorax, however, as Lamming himself acknowledges, is present only by her absence. Lamming hears this silence:

For some reason or other, the memory of Sycorax, Caliban's mother, arouses
him (Prospero) to rage that is almost insane. For all that he is a Duke and noble,
Prospero can't conquer that obscene habit of throwing the past in your face, turning your origins into a weapon of blackmail. In Caliban's case it takes the form of
his mother being a so-and-so.

We ask ourselves why a Duke should debase himself to speak in such a way.
The tone suggests an intimacy of involvement and concern which encourages
speculation. *But we could not speak with authority on the possibilities of this defect until we
had heard from Sycorax and Miranda's mother. They are both dead; and so our knowledge
must be postponed until some arrangement comparable to the Haitian Ceremony of Souls
returns them to tell us what we should and ought to know.* [my emphasis]

Therein lie many of the problems of these societies, for Caliban is
equally the creation of the colonial power that Prospero represents. To
find the true source of authenticity, a more autochthonous lineage or line
of descent, it is to Sycorax we must turn. "This island's mine by Sycorax,
my mother which thou takst from me." Thus Caliban establishes his
rights to the island, but through the mother, the witch Sycorax.

The judgment of Justice Brooks referred to above is a Calibanesque – I
am tempted to say carnivalesque – judgment, as was the attempted coup,
arising out of a society tracing itself only as far back as paper documenta-
tion and writings – European writings – permit. The fear of the unknown, the fear of Sycorax, because she is both female and dark, as in
being both unknown and dark-skinned, is what still holds this piece of
land, these *I-lands* – surrounded by the unknown – in thrall to Europe
and Prospero. While being articulate in Caliban's and so Prospero's
tongue, we are still dumb in the language of Sycorax, whatever that
might be.

The Pleasures of Exile and *A Morning at the Office* became the anchor and
touchstone of my explorations as I traced the labyrinthine patterns colonialism creates, not only in societies but also in the hearts and minds of
the people who are created by them and live in them. My questions – often without answers – wound back in the darkness like some frail string,
back to the source of the pathology that colonialism creates – to some
understanding of what at times appeared to be beyond that very human
need to understand, to make sense of the world and the phenomena that
surround us.

How *does* one begin to make sense of societies where solutions often appear to be worse than the problems; where no one takes responsibility for anything; where people die in public health institutions and those responsible disclaim responsibility; where the release of those who once held a government and its people hostage is heralded as "a proper exercise of the rule of law" (Caliban's language again); where the International Monetary Fund (IMF) has now taken the place of the British Empire in controlling the economies of these islands, purveying and practicing a brand of international monetary terrorism (IMT) masquerading as structural adjustment programs that governments urge their citizens to adopt as "solutions."

But to return to the land – a piece of land – an *I-land* surrounded – Tobago, a tiny island lying to the north and east of Trinidad, presenting the hardworking rural peasant "other" to the urbanized, restless, spendthrift Trinidadian and vice versa. An island as overlooked in recent times as it was fought over in earlier times. Tobago – a piece of land surrounded by the seas of colonialism. Or, perhaps, afloat in its own history.

We could begin in 1986 with a change in government resulting in, among other things, a change in the Alien Landholding Act enabling foreigners to buy and own land in Trinidad and Tobago. This, coupled with a more aggressive thrust in tourism in Tobago, would result in changes to the island, changes which have made Prospero far more prosperous than he ever dreamed. Caliban, in collar and tie and mouthing Prospero's phrases, has also benefited. In little over five years, Prospero and Caliban have between them rapidly recolonized the island – *I-land* – transforming it with the magic of Prospero – white magic – from "a piece of land surrounded by," a piece of land surrounded, to a piece of real estate up for sale to the highest bidder.

We *could* begin in 1986, but the changes mentioned above beginning a long long time ago and we tracing this inability to cherish and treasure what we having, what is fe we own, what we and we ancestors fighting, dying, and working for – the land – back to how we coming here in the first place. Is in the unfortunate relationship the African having with the land here in the Caribbean – on these pieces of land now pieces of real estate – that we finding the reason for this easy easy selling of we place – we own place. Right here on *I-land* where poetry coming to your mouth when you seeing how the land pretty so. But what we must be asking is how those early Africans responding to the land, a land that wherever you turning, you seeing blessing and praise-song and worship in how the sun setting and the sea blue or green, or blue *and* green, and all the growing and giving of the land around you, but the living hard hard so that they not even calling their body their own. Is how you beginning and belonging to a place that belonging to some man in Amsterdam, or Paris, or London, who not seeing the daily beauty of the land; how you beginning and loving a land when the one thing that binding you tight tight in the circle of belonging – your laboring and its fruits – belonging elsewhere; how you beginning and loving a place, a land, "a piece of land surrounded" when everything around and surrounding conspiring and making you alien – stranger to yourself. How, in the words of the spiritual and, later, Marley, you singing your songs in a strange land *to* a strange land. Is in these pickabush questions that we finding the tracings and the spores that Sycorax leaving.

How we belonging to this land? What ownership meaning? Is use we using the Western model of ownership that saying once you owning it you doing what you wanting to do, and to hell with what happening, which resulting in the devastation of the earth that facing us today? Or is it that we closer to how the Native and aboriginal peoples "owning" the land, where one generation holding it in trust for all their future pickney? How we ancestors in Africa owning land? Can we be learning anything there?

This land – this piece of land, an island – *I-land* – causing we so much pain – is the very reason why they bringing we here – to this world – and word – so new in the first place – is how we coming to terms with the pushing and pulling of all that?

Sycorax the witch, the obeah woman, in contest with the magic – the white magic of Prospero – and she saying that after the pain licking you in childbirth and you bringing your pickney to this side, you forgetting how the pain stay once you seeing that pickney and start loving it. But is like we neither forgetting the pain nor loving the pickney – we in no man's lan – a piece of lan – Calibanlan.

In one of his essays, C. L. R. James writing that the Indian in India telling you that the land is his – his father owning it and his grandfather before him and on and on back, but we in the Caribbean, particularly the middle classes, not having this relationship with the land. And Tim Hector the Antiguan intellectual using this argument in his analysis of the Grenadian revolution that failing and falling into brother and sister against brother and sister on a piece of land surrounded by water and the U.S. Marines.

The lacunae in our understanding of our history are profound; it is this that makes it so easy for a repeat of 1492 to happen on this piece of land. Surrounded. A recent development in Tobago underscores this point. Five villas were built on one of most attractive beaches in Black Rock. The villas are upscale and built to resemble colonial architecture, complete with gingerbread trimmings and gabled roofs. They rent for $1,200 U.S. per week. They carry the name Plantation Beach Villas.

For Africans in the New World, the plantation was a machine into which Europeans fed the raw material of African laborers, most of whom did not survive it. Replacement by other Africans was often the source of labor here in the Caribbean; or, where they could, owners bred new workers. In other words, the "plantation" equaled death for the African. It meant the destruction of families and all the social integuments that bind a people together.

The plantation for the European no doubt conjures up tropical Rhett Butlers and Scarlett O'Haras sipping the Caribbean equivalent of mint juleps—rum punches. Whose reality? Whose history? In whose name do we open up this "piece of land surrounded by" to the foreigners, even as we embrace, since that appears to be our desire, our erstwhile masters? Their name or ours? Would, for instance, Israelis allow anyone to build "Concentration Camp Cabins" on the Dead Sea? Why are we so cavalier with our history, both large and small?

"Plantation" is not "just a name" as some have argued. How could it be, when the owners of this very "plantation" are planting bushes around the swimming pool because they "don't want the *natives* looking at the people swimming." *Plantation* can never be "just a word." Not on this piece of land. It hangs differently on us than on Europeans and we have earned the right to object strongly and strenuously to its use in a context that merely serves to replicate what it originally meant for us. What is, in fact, happening is that Caliban is trying to inhabit the word in the same way the Europeans do.

Plantation Beach Villas are all of a piece with the development of a settler society that is integral to any colonization process, and Tobago is no exception. Where previously you had a predominantly black population with a sprinkling of local whites—creole families who belonged by dura-

tion and the creolization that came from intermingling – you now have
expatriates owning a piece of a piece of land. They come, the Germans,
the Americans, the English, the Canadians, buying their choice pieces of
real estate. They come because they like the land, the laid-back quality
of the island, yet they spend much of their time complaining about everything – from schooling to repairmen to domestics. Tobagonians for their
part are impressed that they are being noticed. Finally. Some express
pride at the fact that "Germans are coming to live here," not seeming to
know or care about Germany's past record toward Jews, Africans, and
other non-Aryans, not to mention its present record against peoples of
color. Having been ignored for so long, is it that *any* attention is better
than none? Particularly from Europeans and Americans? Has there been
any attempt to encourage African Americans to buy or invest in Tobago,
for instance?

Others predict with great satisfaction that in twenty years the place
will be run by Indians, Germans, and Americans, because "they all work
harder than our people."

The first and most noticeable effect of this European and American
incursion – invasion? – is the driving up of the price of land so that local
people are now unable to own a piece of their piece of land – their
I-land – surrounded. Alongside this is an attitude toward the local
Tobagonian that can be summed up in one word: contempt. It is palpable
and can be heard in their comments about every aspect of the island.
Like settlers always have, they do not involve themselves in any aspect of
island life that is an expression of the people, and yet they live here,
clinging relentlessly to each other, their shared and mutual prejudices,
and their racism.

Essentially, what is happening is a repeat of Columbus all over again –
they come, they covet, they conquer. So, for instance, a large tract of land
is bought on the northern coast and, shortly after, signs appear declaring
it a nature preserve (not under the auspices of the government); users of
the beach are warned not to remove *anything*, not even coconut branches.
For whom is the area being "preserved," and *from* whom? Surely the pur-
chaser would not have bought this piece of a piece of land had he, she, or
they not seen something they liked and valued – something, in fact, that
had been cared for enough to make it desirable. Which is not to say that
there isn't room for great improvement in preservation of forests and

woodlands and their inhabitants. But, like Columbus, the first response of the Western buyer to his ownership is exclusion and condemnation, either directly or by implication, of those who originally held or used the land before. The motto seems to be *Come, buy, exclude.* So much so that recently a member of the Tobago House of Assembly was quoted as saying that the Assembly had to find ways to ensure that Tobagonians had access to their beaches. This, in a country where the laws already provide that people must have access to all beachfronts.

And so to return to *I-land* – a piece of land where I and my parents and their parents before them were born – surrounded by the seas – Caribbean and Atlantic; a piece of real estate coveted now as it was five hundred years ago by the Europeans (and their American descendants). A piece of land that is not yet a land of peace.

After thirty years of constitutional independence crafted by Caliban, the most radical idea for most people in Caribbean societies – black and white and those in between – is still that black people ought to be controlling their own lives. As George Lamming recently said, "the legacy of fear (left by colonials) created and nourished by an ideology of racism has never been overcome to this day. Adult suffrage and the black composition of the political directorate have not succeeded in disturbing a profound conviction among black Barbadians that the white economic elite are the natural and most reliable custodians of that island's destiny" (*Express*, November 21, 1991). While Tobago is not the same as Barbados, I concur with Lamming that the distortion of values mentioned above is found in varying degrees throughout the Caribbean. Tobago has not escaped it; the rapid changes it is presently going through in a relatively short space of time is, in fact, leading to a further distortion and warping of values.

We began by being a European idea and we continue to shape our ideas by European models since we fear the darkness of Sycorax and the questions she poses. We, in Tobago, on this piece of land surrounded, this *I-land,* we in Trinidad *and* Tobago, we in the Caribbean, have suffered an abject failure of the imagination – of the past. No better example of the failure of imagination is the above mentioned judgment concerning the Muslimeen. The occasion presented by the habeas corpus application ought to have created an opportunity for us to grapple with the kind of society we want – examining the source of law, whose own harsh application society must often mitigate. We do not yet understand that laws do not exist in a vacuum but form a part of society, and that in bequeathing us and Caliban his laws, Prospero was also passing on the values of a system riddled with class prejudices, a system in which the law was but a tool of the governing classes. A system in which the law attempted to transform the African from human to thing—chattel, *meuble*, *cosa*—to be bought and sold at will. I say "attempted to" because, while the law did specify the African's "thingness," it was helpless in the face of the essential humanity of the African; song, music, dance, poetry, spirituality—all these expressions of culture and, therefore, humanness, which the law attempted time and again to stifle and eradicate, pointed to the unassailable African genius.

When is it allowed for a people to take up arms against its government? When does a government lose its validity, its authority, which it must always get from the people? The failure of the legal system—for it is not simply a failure of one individual—to deal with these questions, its reliance on narrow legalism, is evidence that what we have is a legal system, and *not* a system of laws that are the outgrowth of a people struggling to define itself, its place, its *I-land*.

The fact that the privy council came to a decision that appeared to run counter to what may be in the best interests of the nation, not to mention its strong intimation of how the habeas corpus application *ought* to be decided, should not surprise us: colonial governments have been notorious for making decisions that were of no benefit, or ran counter to, the best interests of the colony. All of which is not to say that our legal system does not need to be reformed, refurbished, if not scrapped entirely and rebuilt from the ground up. Part of the reason for the present state of the justice system lies in its genealogy and how and why Prospero passed it to Caliban. But that is another issue. Only an independent and self-governing people will undertake to look at it honestly.

Sycorax continues to terrify us with her witchcraft and obeah; our powers of re/membering the future have atrophied. Hence the ease with which we sell our birthright, our *I-land*, to the highest bidder.

The "piece of land surrounded by" that is Tobago is unique in that it suffers a double colonialism process—via Europe and via Trinidad. In many respects Trinidad's relationship with Tobago mirrors England's earlier relationship with its colonies, with the latter having very little control over their affairs.

The University of the West Indies, which ought to have been carrying the beacon of developing a new language, new modes of knowing, new knowing vis-à-vis knowledge, has failed us. But it has always been the people, not the institutions, who have been the caretakers of all that is valuable in our culture, and on them falls the burden of re/membering the future.

A piece of land – a piece of real estate surrounded by water. Or, a piece of land floating – keeping itself afloat consciously, responsibly, and responsively. Island or *I-land*, or *I'n I land*. Sycorax *and* Caliban or Caliban alone. That is the stark choice facing us on *I-land* today – it permeating every activity while Prospero continuing and working his white magic. The next five hundred years showing whether we equal to the challenge and calling Sycorax to living through the Ceremony of Souls, or whether we continuing and letting Caliban perform his macabre dance in the shadow of Prospero.

A L I S O N   D E M I N G

The Nature of Poetry: Poetry in Nature

[DOWNEAST POETRY WORKSHOP]

Lately I have been trying to attend to nature in a careful fashion, trying to strip away my conscious preconceptions and to listen for the most forceful statements that nature might make to me. My motive has been to get away from seeing nature as the idealized other, and human beings as the dysfunctionals of the natural world. I have been looking for a more integrated view that admits that chaos and destruction, and moral and aesthetic order, exist everywhere in nature, that these forces are embedded in us, as we are embedded in the ecosystem. We don't yet know nearly enough about nature – it truly is an inexhaustible mystery. I have come up with three recent observations that I will summarize with three talismanic phrases: hanta virus, bald eagle, 111 degrees. Let me elaborate.

During the spring of 1993 at least eighteen people died, many of them young and healthy, most of them living in Navajo lands in northern New Mexico and Arizona. An unknown disease, flulike and rapid, has taken them. The public health detectives and the tribal medicine people have puzzled and postulated, working intently to find and allay the cause. Several theories have been floated, but the most likely is that a new strain of hanta virus spread by rodent droppings has evolved in the area. The tribal elders suspected the disease was related to piñon nuts, which have been much more bountiful than usual this year due to a winter of record-high rainfall. Since desert rodents thrive on piñons, deer mice and pack rats have been bountiful as well, thereby increasing the possibility of contact with people. Nature, this phenomenon reminds me, is ceaselessly improvising, adopting new forms that incorporate the available material. Nature has no sympathy for individuals, no preference among species. Everything is food for fodder (including young and hearty members of the apparently dominant species) in the great collective appetite of evolution.

I recently attended a symposium in Alaska at which I was swept into the white water of collective thinking about our relatedness to nature and the precarious waterfall toward which our species intently paddles. Between the heady sessions (How can we get loggers and environmentalists to talk to one another? How can we reimagine our innocence?), I'd walk outside to watch bald eagles cruise the sky, this one calling to its mate, another carrying in its talons a two-foot-long twig to tuck in its nest in the high crown of a Sitka spruce. The paradox was not lost to me that I had flown thousands of miles – paying a huge corporation to consume fossil fuels and dump their rank residue into the atmosphere – so that I could watch eagles and speculate about right relationship with nature. This is how all of our problems look these days – everything is embedded in everything else so that the degree of complication makes us feel hopeless. It's "their" fault, we say – the loggers, the Republicans, the capitalists, the philistines. And yet when we look soberly at our own appetites and habits, each of us is a strand in the tangled web. Our problems are as delicately interwoven as are the relationships among ourselves and the microbes that live in our guts. Nature – the biotic community of earth – in all its beauty, complexity, ugliness, violence, and versatility *is* connectedness. Connectedness is *our* nature. Yet we never satisfy our hunger for connectedness with one another or with our own fleeting experience. We are nature hungering for itself.

When I returned home to Arizona, the temperature was 106 and everyone reported how it had peaked a few days earlier at 111. My five California sycamores had gone into a leaf-drop that looked like fall. Suffering from the heat, the dryness, and an opportunistic infestation of white flies, they looked desperate and out of place. I called the tree doctor, who drilled cores into the trunks, sinking implants of insecticide and iron into the wood. Sycamores really are out of place in Tucson. They prefer to grow at higher elevations and nearer to constant water. Here they must

endure six months without a drop of rain and under the beating of fero-
cious sunlight. But given some modest attention, they manage to live and
to provide a flickering canopy of leaves over my side yard that would be
difficult to part with. By contrast, the paloverde is well adapted to this
fierce climate and its survival strategy is a testament to the entrepreneur-
ial nature of nature. Having broad leaves in the desert is not a good idea,
because surface area increases the evaporation of precious moisture. The
paloverde has solved this problem by developing long needlelike leaves
that conserve water. The delicate needles, however, do not provide
enough chlorophyll for efficient photosynthesis, so the tree has developed green bark, enabling it to photosynthesize all along its trunk and
branches. This seems stunningly intelligent to me and testifies that, at
least here in the Sonoran Desert, the land's desire to produce vegetation
is too passionate to be quelled by mere centuries of drought. Nature displays such unlikely persistence in numerous inhospitable habitats.

What does this have to do with poetry? I think it has everything to do
with poetry, since the art is quite simply another of the products of the
natural world, and one of the more honorably humble products of our
species. As John Haines writes, "there is nothing in the *mind*, this imagination, this capacity for thought, that does not find its source, its example
and inspiration, in the natural world. . . . [Nature] is, to say it yet another
way, the great book we have been reading, and writing, from the beginning." And the three characteristics of nature that my recent observations
yielded seem particularly apt to a discussion of poetry. First, poetry *is* the
invention (and reinvention) of form using what materials are available.
Forms evolve as our sense of reality changes, capturing a glimmer of the
shape of the mental and emotional experience characteristic of a given
time in history. As Adrienne Rich writes, "I don't want to know / wreck-
age, dreck and waste, but these are the materials." Second, poetry is an
expression of our hunger for connectedness. We write to cross the borders that separate us from others. And in the solitary process of writing,
we feel selflessly connected to an ideal reader, or as Charles Wright said
it, to the better part of ourselves. And third, poetry displays an unlikely
persistence in a culture that is, at best, indifferent to it. To put it metaphorically, poetry is the stubborn grass that grows between the cracks in
the sidewalk.

One of our most dangerous post-European cultural beliefs is that we are separate from nature, exiled from the instinctual paradise of natural order and balance. I don't mean that we are incapable of experiencing the beauty of coastal marsh grass or the grace of a breaching humpback. I mean that immediately after those ecstatic encounters in which we exclaim "Look at that!" to our companions, there is a sigh of dismay or grief. The lives of plants and animals seem blessed by survival instincts, while our lives (examined as a planetary phenomenon) seem to be a disaster. We know our species to be greedy, genocidal, warmongering, wasteful, and apparently incapable of serving as custodians of the future. We are the ones who have thrown nature out of balance. We need no further evidence that this is the case. And we can no longer run away from our ruin in search of new wilderness – that great American story that our ancestors carried with them from Europe. That story is over. We need a new one. Are we smart enough to reimagine ourselves? I don't know. No one knows. This is the essential tension and question of our time.

John Haines also has said that there is no progress in nature or in art. I think that he is right. John Ashbery's "Self-Portrait in a Convex Mirror" does not supersede the cave paintings at Lascaux. We do not supersede the dinosaurs. Each being, each period of flowering and decay, is nature's patient response to the circumstances of the time. When something goes wrong in nature (a volcano or asteroid spewing debris into space and darkening the sun), species die out. We are the first creatures to know that this has happened to other species and may happen to us – *will*, eventually, undoubtedly happen to us and to everything on Earth when the Sun in its death throes goes supernova. This physical ending of life on Earth is the toughest metaphysical challenge, since most of us lack a faith sufficient to protect us from even our individual deaths. We make art and things that proclaim loudly, "I am here! I have substance!" But we lack a story of who we are that would make us feel at home in our skins. Our faith in nature is insufficient. We believe it will be a moral failure if our species goes extinct. But nature will simply be clearing the way for the next invention, opening a new blank notebook – or, more accurately, reworking the notes it has taken thus far. How do we live with the complexity our lives have become?

I think poems and stories can help. From Aesop's fables to *Jurassic*

Park, we have looked to nature, and especially to the lives of animals, to teach us about moral order. And if we lack anything, it is a clear sense of moral order. James Merrill speaks of:

> Stories whose glow we see our lives bathed in –
> The mere word "animal" a skin
> Through which its old sense glimmers, *of the soul*.

So I want to move on now to talking about some poems that offer that glimmer and that I believe have something to contribute in terms of reimagining ourselves, not as the dysfunctionals of the natural world but as its custodians. Whatever we believe about nature and ourselves is always a story, a version of the truth as told by a specific narrator. Art should be helpful, useful. It should enhance our ability to commit acts of will when they are required. And reimagining ourselves clearly requires acts of will.

In *Leaves of Grass* Walt Whitman writes:

> I think I could turn and live with the animals, they are
>   so placid and self-contained,
> I stand and look at them sometimes an hour at a stretch.
>
> They do not sweat and whine about their condition,
> They do not lie awake in the dark and weep for their
>   sins,
> They do not make me sick discussing their duty to
>   God,
> Not one is dissatisfied – not one is demented with the
>   mania of owning things,
> Not one kneels to another, nor to his kind that lived
>   thousands of years ago,
> Not one is respectable or industrious over the whole
>   earth.

This excerpt *celebrates* the split of which I've spoken – that human beings are essentially separate from nature and animal beings. I love the poem for its longing for the innocence of animal life and for its critique of human malcontent and striving. Whitman even ridicules our more noble pipe dreams – to be respectable and industrious – because, I infer, our striving is so ceaseless and judgment-laden. The poem seems to say that we are an error in nature – or at least that we lack the equanimity with our own natures that animals personify. The poem idealizes animals for their very lack of moral responsibility.

Rather than separating human beings from animal beings, hence from nature, Chilean poet and activist Cecilia Vicuña writes an equation in which *poem* equals *animal*. The poem in its entirety reads:

> The poem is the animal
>
> Sinking its mouth
> in the stream

She defines the animal moment specifically and lyrically. It is important to note that it is not the *poet* sinking *her* mouth in the stream – but the *poem* itself that has gained a life of its own, become *animated* as a creature in the natural world, a product of evolution, and must quench its thirst.

I've separated (how human of me) the remaining poems I want to talk about into three groups. The first are poems of natural observation in which the author pays careful attention to an animal behavior. In this fashion, the work has something in common with the field notebook of a natural scientist – but the poems tend to move from observation to drawing some lesson about how we ought to live.

Greg Pape's poem "The Jackrabbit's Ears" begins with a fable-like question, similar to Kipling's *Just-So Stories.*

> Why do jackrabbits have such big ears?
> I always thought it was because
> they liked to sit in the shade
> of a creosote bush or a juniper
> all day and listen to God
> or whatever devil might be hungry
> and headed their way.
> That's what I do when I sit
> at the desk waiting for the spirit
> to move me, looking for words
> to say whatever it is that needs

to be said. I envy the jackrabbit
his patience and his instinct.

I admire his big ears, ears
the light passes through, ears
that radiate the heat of his body
and cool him without loss
of water, ears he holds erect
at an angle of seventeen degrees
from the north horizon, pointed
precisely at the coolest area of sky,
listening for the exact sound
of the present, and for the life ahead.

Pape's critter lives in a real, geographic terrain where there are creo-
sote and juniper bushes. His observations are precise – right down to the
exact angle at which the rabbit's ears incline to pick up a distant sound.
But this jackrabbit also lives on a moral ground where God and devils are
forces in its life. Pape equates the rabbit's ears and how well evolved they
are for their job with the poet's imagination. The poem thereby dignifies
the animal and humbles the human. In this leveling assessment, it offers
a postcolonial, post-Columbian view of nature.

Rodney Jones, like Whitman, speaks of the characteristic differences
between human and animal beings in "Shame the Monsters." Unlike
Whitman, who ridicules his own kind and would like to send us back in
evolutionary time to some state of pure instinctual bliss, Jones takes on
the complexity and vulnerability of our current inner lives and dilemmas.

It is good, after all, to pause and lick one's genitalia
To hunch one's shoulders and gag, regurgitating lunch,
To mark one's curb and grass, to bay when the future beckons
        from the nose,
Not to exhaust so much of the present staring into the flat
        face of a machine
Not to spend so much of the logic and the voice articulating
        a complex whimper of submission,
But to run with a full stomach under the sun, to play in the
        simple water and to wallow oneself dry in the leaves,

To take the teeth in the neck, if it comes to that,
If it comes to little and lean and silent, to take the
    position of the stone, even to hide under the stone,
But not to ride up the spine of the building with acid
    scalding the gut,
Not to sit at a long table, wondering
How not to howl when the tall one again personifies the
    organization. . . .

While Jones critiques our technological and organizational ways, he makes at least this reader feel a tenderness toward our human limitations. When he opens the second stanza with the entreaty, "Dear Mammals, help me, the argument with the flesh is too fierce. . ." he seems to say that he loves us all for our animal need for one another. The poem closes with these stunning lines:

Better to take the mud in the hands and holler for no reason,
    to praise the strange
Alchemy of mud and rain: there is sex; there is food.
It is good to say anything in the spirit of hair and breasts
    and warm blood,
And not to deny the private knowledge, not to wonder how not
    to speak of death,
And not to deny the knowledge of death, not to invent the
    silence,
Not to wonder how not to say the words of love.

By opening the poem with the unself-conscious behavior of animals licking their genitalia and ending with the difficulties of human love, Jones frames the evolutionary distance we have come. I'm touched by the ambivalent nature of that last line in which, speaking of how different the animals are from us, how much better their lives are in many ways — "It is good . . . / not to wonder how not to say the words of love." I don't fully understand what he means by that. I make two possible readings — perhaps there are others. It's true that we sometimes must "wonder how not to say the words of love." We do it when we resist an inappropriate love or desire for someone. And even more puzzling, when we avoid saying "I love you" to someone because we fear the vulnerability we may experience. What if so-and-so does not return my love? What if so-and-so is frightened away by my frank statement of emotion? The line speaks with insight about our mysterious and complicated emotions and needs. Perhaps a third reading hints back to the preceding lines—when one has lost a loved one to death, how can one stop expressing one's intimate connection? The poem does not ask us to return to idealized instinctual ways. It obliquely asks us, I think, to understand and forgive ourselves, while we ironically "shame the monsters."

The second grouping of poems speaks of our moral responsibility to nature, or looks for a sense of moral order drawn from phenomena in nature. Mary Oliver's poem "Spring" gives the reader not an observed bear, but an imagined one.

> Somewhere
>   a black bear
>   has just risen from sleep
>   and is staring
>
> down the mountain.
>   All night
>   in the brisk and shallow restlessness
>   of early spring
>
> I think of her,
>   her four black fists
>   flicking the gravel,
>   her tongue
>
> like a red fire
>   touching the grass,
>   the cold water.
>   There is only one question:
>
> how to love this world. . . .

By opening with the word "somewhere," the poet lets the reader know that what follows is speculation in the head, rather than observation in the field. This is an imagined bear and the poem reminds us first of the importance of *bear* in our imaginations. What would happen to our waking and dreaming consciousness if there were no such a thing as *bear?* In what ways would our lives be diminished? The poem states that our failure is quite simply a failure of love. Oliver's gift is to see the natural world with a simplicity that seems obvious, but which most of us are too confused or too busy to see without her help. The question is simple: "How to love this world," even if the answers are not readily apparent. This ability to love the world, the poem suggests, is the spring we should hope for – to reimagine ourselves as purely loving.

"Arson" by David Romtvedt is, again, a poem of careful and accurate observation of the natural world – the field notebook approach.

> At work we found a rattler.
> The job was to make a rip-rap
> on the desert as if waves
> would someday reach that sea. But it was
> only to stop erosion so men could stand on artifical
> mounds to fire their guns across the air. I don't
> remember thinking the snake would strike. I can't
> remember any fear or idea that I wanted
> to take action. I didn't say a word when another boy
> said, "We have to kill it" and no one disagreed. So we
> did it with stones, at the end striking its head
> like hammering nails to hold targets, hanging
> on to the stone. Then an older man slit its belly
> open, throat to tail, telling stories about other rattlers,
> scrambled eggs and snake brains, being alone
> on the desert. He uncoiled nine unborn snakes, eyes
> still creamlike membrane. They tried to wind themselves
> back round, moving from side to side. It may be they
> were alive or if not, all tropism, some dead creature's
> dance of nerve endings and light. I must not have asked,
> must not have said a thing, just
> looked, learning that rattlesnakes are born
> one at a time: the unwinding of the young
> on the flat surface of a stone
> where they sizzle and pop in the faultless sun.

The poem clearly takes place in a fallen world. Men are building a platform or stone cobble on an artillery range. They all agree to the "necessary killing" of a rattlesnake – though there is no apparent threat from this specific creature. It is a generic response to the animal. The author participates as heartily as any of the boys with whom he works and kills. But an insight comes when he sees the pearly baby snakes unwind from the mother snake's slit belly. The little ones wriggle and die on the hot stone. As the author observes this he realizes that "rattlesnakes are born / one at a time," each genetically programmed, neurologically tuned to *want* its life. This insight about the specificity of an individual snake serves as a kind of moral antidote to the generic killing. All that's faultless here is the sun. Until the last line – "where they sizzle and pop in the faultless sun" – we don't know the significance of the title, "Arson." The baby snakes die in the heat of the sun. The sun does the burning, but the speaker rightly claims moral responsibility for the crime.

The next group of poems are works that offer metaphysical speculation about our relationship with nature, poems that willfully work at asking us to reimagine ourselves. First is William Stafford's "Evolution:"

> The thing is, I'm still
> an animal. What is a spirit,
> I wonder. But I only wonder:
> I'll never know.
>
> Night comes and I'm hungry.
> Tempted by anything, or called
> by my peculiar appetites,
> I turn aside, faithfully.
>
> What comes before me
> transforms into my life.
> "Truth," I say, and it answers,
> "I'm what you need."
>
> I sing, and a song shaped like a bird
> flies out of my mouth.

The speaker acknowledges that he is an animal, a moral being, a product and agent of evolution. He has no apparent conflict about his nature. The physical and the spiritual seem balanced and harmonious in this

speaker. It is an amazingly unified and peaceful vision of self. He unifies
poetry and nature by suggesting that both are means of energy transformation: "What comes before me / transforms into my life." It reminds
me of Muriel Rukeyser's beautiful lines: "Breathe in experience, /
breathe out poetry." The passage places the act of poetry making securely in the biological domain. And the poet's song, "shaped like a
bird," flying out of his mouth, is an act of creation as tangible and as in-
tangible as the pigeons a magician might pull from his cape.

Pattiann Rogers works the nexus between science and spirituality in a
way unique among U.S. poets. She refuses to let her rich scientific
knowledge rob her of a sense of celebration and wonder. Her work is informed and inspired by the cosmology of the late twentieth century – and
her language draws beautifully from scientific research and discourse.
She begins in "Supposition" with the physical:

> Suppose the molecular changes taking place
> In the mind during the act of praise
> Resulted in an emanation rising into space.
> Suppose that emanation went forth
> In the configuration of its occasion:
> For instance, the design of rain pocks
> On the lake's surface or the blue depths
> Of the canyon with its horizontal cedars stunted.
>
> Suppose praise had physical properties
> And actually endured? What if the pattern
> Of its disturbances rose beyond the atmosphere,
> Becoming a permanent outline implanted in the cosmos –
> The sound of the celebratory banjo or horn
> Lodging near the third star of Orion's belt;
> Or to the east of the Pleiades, an atomic
> Disarrangement of the words,
> "How particular, the pod-eyed hermit crab
> And his prickly orange legs"?
>
> Suppose benevolent praise,
> Coming into being by our will,
> Had a separate existence, its purple or azure light

Gathering in the upper reaches, affecting
The aura of morning haze over autumn fields,
Or causing a perturbation in the mode of an asteroid.
What if praise and its emanations
Were necessary catalysts to the harmonious
Expansion of the void? Suppose, for the prosperous
Welfare of the universe, there were an element
Of need involved.

We know from neuroscience that the molecules of the brain *do* physically change to incorporate a new idea or memory. Rogers turns that knowledge around to suppose that our ideas and emotions might physically change the universe. In a preposterous and visionary claim, she speculates that our very purpose might be to infuse the cosmos with praise. We are factories of the tangible stuff called praise. It is a fuel, she postulates, that energizes the very expansion of the universe. Our consciousness has evolved as food for that cosmic hunger. This vision marries contemporary scientific lore with the prior theological notion that God needs us as partners for Creation.

Finally, I'd like to close with a discursive and rhapsodic passage from "The Kingdom of Poetry" by Delmore Schwartz. Written in the forties, the poem predates our contemporary doubts about language and our chronic insecurity about the efficacy of our art. He is an ecstatic here and the poem offers a kind of mental equivalent to the gold-lit landscapes of Frederic Church, Thomas Cole, and Asher Duran. Schwartz launches the poem with its title, placing "The Kingdom of Poetry" right beside the two other great earthly kingdoms—those of the plants and of the animals. He brings a rapture to the subject that seamlessly unifies poetry and nature, and accounts for that experience of unity in a reinvention of innocence and its inherent attentiveness.

For it is true that poetry invented the unicorn, the centaur,
    and the phoenix.
Hence it is true that poetry is an everlasting Ark,
An omnibus containing, bearing and begetting all the mind's
    animals.
Whence it is that poetry gave and gives tongue to forgiveness
Therefore a history of poetry would be a history of joy, and

a history of the mystery of love
For poetry provides spontaneously, abundantly and freely
The petnames and the diminutives which love requires and
    without which the mystery of love cannot be mastered.

For poetry is like light, and it is light.
It shines over all, like the blue sky, with the same blue
    justice.
For poetry is the sunlight of consciousness:
It is also the soil of the fruits of knowledge
       In the orchards of being:
    It shows us the pleasures of the city.
    It lights up the structures of reality.
    It is a cause of knowledge and laughter:
    It sharpens the whistles of the witty:
    It is like morning and the flutes of morning, chanting
       and enchanted.
    It is the birth and rebirth of the first morning
       forever.

CHARLES BAXTER

Talking Forks: Fiction and the Inner Life of Objects

[WARREN WILSON COLLEGE]

For Irving Massey

About a third of the way through Ivan Turgenev's second novel, *Home of the Gentry* (1859), the hero, a luckless man named Lavretsky who has been experiencing a painful marriage and who will soon fall in love with a woman as unsuited to him as his wife has been, pauses for a moment to observe the flow of natural events outside in an open field. Lavretsky, we are to understand, has not been a particularly gifted observer at any time in his life, at least until now. His slight taint of obtuseness probably accounts for his tendency to love people who cannot love him back.

Because this is a Russian novel of the mid-nineteenth century, Lavretsky's gift of sight occurs on an estate. He is between scenes and is feeling bored and lazy. For the first time, it seems, he is paying some attention to things he cannot touch or eat. (The narrative has somewhat slyly let us know that he is overweight.) Feeling calmly indolent in the middle of his unharvested crops, he begins to listen to gnats and bees. Half lost in all the vegetation, he sees brightly burnished rye and the oats that have formed (in Richard Freeborn's translation for the Penguin edition) "their little trumpet ears." Out of habit, he returns his conscious attention to himself and thinks immediately of his miserable romantic attachments, but then, as if his perspective has been subtly adjusted, he looks again at the objects in front of him.

All at once the sounds die, and Lavretsky is "engulfed" in silence. He looks up and sees "the tranquil blue of the sky, and the clouds floating silently upon it; it seemed as if they knew why and where they were going."

Russian literature is rich in moments when wisdom arises out of indolence, but this one seems unusually eerie to me. Lavretsky has lost his industry, or rather his industriousness, and in this pre-industrious state he can see self-contradicting objects that are metaphorically both ears and trumpets, producers and receivers of sound that are playing only in his imagination. In his laziness, Lavretsky gives up his feeling and thinking to the objects that constitute his environment, and in this air pocket of silence the clouds acquire consciousness and a sort of ontological intelligence. The passing of the clouds feels slightly god-haunted, although no god is visible anywhere in the scene.

It seems important to me to resist reading this episode through what we may know about Wordsworth or English Romantic poetry, or epiphanies, or psychoanalysis and Zen Buddhism. The twentieth century has built up a powerful set of intellectual shortcuts and devices that help us defend ourselves against moments when clouds suddenly appear to think. To say that clouds know something is already to sound a little mad. Lavretsky has given away some of his emotional and intellectual autonomy, and suddenly the things surrounding him have their own thoughts and feelings – not necessarily Lavretsky's – and in this reduction of the human scale, Lavretsky's misery disappears. Lavretsky has momentarily recognized an integrity in nature that was invisible as long as he made himself gigantic with pain and problems. Lavretsky's misery will reappear because the plot demands it, but this moment will function as a benchmark – at least for the reader, if not for Lavretsky – against which to measure the size of his feelings.

In this century, the fiction with which we have grown familiar has tended to insist on the insentience and thoughtlessness of things, if not their outright malevolence. Generally things have no presence at all except as barriers or rewards for human endeavor. When nature is given something like a face to look back at humans, as it often is in Conrad's stories and novels, the expression on that face is typically one of straightforward hostility. Or at least what seems to be hostility: the violence of

nature – its typhoons and uninterpretable remoteness – is what nature
flings back at men who are deeply involved in the project of imperialism.
If, as Conrad often insists, imperialism is a kind of rape of nature, then it
should be no surprise that man's violence is visited upon him in return,
coming the other way as a force field of unknowingness, the "sullen,
dumb, menacing hostility," for example, that Lena perceives in the forest in *Victory*. This often leaves Conrad's characters in a highly specified
nowhere where the only option is not to grant objects much visibility of
any kind, as in Winnie Verloc's repeated assertion in *The Secret Agent* that
"most things did not bear very much looking into."

I want to trouble this topic because I think that contemporary fiction has
gradually been developing a fascinated relationship with objects that par-
allels in some respects the concerns of the ecological movement. It is as if
things are again, after a war of about eighty years, making visible a correspondence to human feelings, but only under certain circumstances. The
truce, if there is one, is probably conditional. To say that the realms of
objects and humans may be collaborative, however, is to risk an obvious
sentimentalism in the face of continued human violence against the
earth; and to say that things may be "making visible a correspondence to
human feelings" still sounds slightly mad and wrongfully acquisitive.
John Ruskin's concept of the pathetic fallacy is deeply implicated in such
responses.

Madness, like many conditions, has to be culturally defined, and one
can see a part of that definition being formulated in Ruskin's delineation
of the pathetic fallacy in 1856. In this essay, Ruskin takes it upon himself
to define what he calls an "unhinged" literary response to nature by ana-
lyzing certain metaphors that writers employ. What Ruskin asserted as an
aesthetic working principle became an informal aesthetic law in the
twentieth century. My interest here is not so much to argue against that
law as to ask how it came into existence in the first place.

Things, Ruskin says, should not be made to reflect the emotions of
the observer. In poetry and prose, human emotions should not be allowed to discolor the integrity of observed phenomena. Although Ruskin
would not have put it this way, his objection is to an overspillage of
human expression onto the things that surround the individual. Ruskin's

claim in this chapter of *Modern Painters* that the projection of human feel-ings on things is fallacious, untrue, morbid, and frightful has all the vio-lence of an ideology that is meant to put certain kinds of poets in their place. His examples are interesting. One is two lines from a poem by Oli-ver Wendell Holmes:

> The spendthrift crocus, bursting through the mold
> Naked and shivering, with his cup of gold.

Curiously enough, Ruskin does not object to "naked and shivering" but to "spendthrift." The crocus, he says, is *not* spendthrift but "hardy." It does not give away, apparently, but instead hoards. Ruskin finds the poem's metaphor for the plant's economic life mistaken and, as he says, "untrue." But in eliminating one metaphor for plant life – "spendthrift" – Ruskin substitutes another metaphor – "hardy" – without appearing to recognize that the inescapability of metaphors and figurative language is part of the problem that he is trying to correct. Evidently the crocus is more like a young Victorian gentleman or banker than an undisciplined and sentimental squanderer of a fortune.

In another example, from a novel by Charles Kingsley, Ruskin quotes with considerable distaste the phrase "cruel, crawling foam" and argues that as a phrase it is "unhinged." Of course Ruskin's point is clear enough. He is simply observing that when people say that the "storm is raging," for example, there is no real rage in the storm. The rage is human and is projected upon the storm. Human attributes cross a bound-ary line and are wrongfully stitched to the nonhuman.

In his pleasantly irascible way, Ruskin is doing his best to define a problem that is considerably larger than he is. He is describing the distor-tion of perceptions that (he believes) occurs when someone has what he calls "violent feelings." Violent feelings, he says, produce a "falseness in all our impressions of external things." Feelings, or as he says, "souls," can be compared to things, but the separateness of the feelings and the things must be maintained; in his opinion Dante maintains this distance but Coleridge does not. The result is what Ruskin calls a "morbid" effect in Coleridge. The world's integrity can be saved (by implication) through the deployment of a discriminating sensibility.

At certain times of day, Ruskin's love of sanity is lovable, as is his hope
that the worlds of human consciousness and nature can be made figuratively distinct. Behind his anger is a certain understandable squeamish-
ness, a distaste for any kind of aesthetic confusion. He desires clarity.
And there is a sense also behind his words that he is entering a battle that
he suspects he is going to lose. Ruskin sees nature being entered,
mucked around with, and violated for the purposes of what he thinks is
second-rate poetry – cheap effects and paltry lyricism.

Everywhere Ruskin looks, he sees the human presence expanding.
Objects are being shamelessly taken over, *used*, for an easy poetical effect, which is imperialism at the level of aesthetics. Objects are being
forced to go to work, are being *employed* to carry their burden of human
feeling. No one is leaving objects alone anymore – not in industry, or in
literature. Ruskin wants to stop this expansionism and confusion of
realms, but he has to do so by bracketing violent feelings and the atroci-
ties that give rise to them and putting them to the side somewhere. In a
rather English manner, he seems to want to deny that when people look
at things, things look back. He is thus resisting both emotional violence
and the Being that gazes out from objects. His assumption is that all emotional violence arises out of sensationalism and a carelessness in the nota-
tion of feeling. For him, emotional confusion is by its very nature violent.
All this, as I have said, is understandable and even lovable, and it has the
sound of someone sitting in a comfortable study and saying that there will
be no war, there must not be a war, even as the guns of the twentieth century start blasting away, and the terms of the war are announced by the
John-the-Baptist of apocalypse, Friedrich Nietzsche.

Ruskin's essay on the pathetic fallacy takes its place in a larger quarrel
about the division of literary property in the nineteenth century. At about
the time of the rise of the English novel, a marker or borderline begins to
appear in literary consciousness that makes the relationship between the
inner life of human beings and the inner life of objects almost exclusively
a matter for poetry. It is as if all the speaking about the terms of the relationship between people and the spirit within things will occur in poetry
and poetics or in almost uncategorizable writing such as theosophy. We
begin to hear about these matters from Wordsworth and Baudelaire,
Rilke and Yeats and Vallejo, Madame Blavatsky and Rudolf Steiner.

(Steiner's observations that anyone can intuit an individual spirit poking the water upward underneath each wave, or that there are some experiences that make the mind resemble an anthill, travel so far beyond the pathetic fallacy that, in his writing, philosophy demands a religious leap of faith.)

Virtually all myths, fables, and allegories assert that there is an inner life to things – that things speak to us – but with the advance of science and historical materialism, to say nothing of commercial culture, the life of objects is defined as either poetic or surreal or a base-line assumption of insanity. In the case of Marx, the only life an object has consists of its life as a commodity, tossed back and forth in the tidal ebb and flow of capital. By the late nineteenth century, it is as if the division of realms has become absolute: poetry gets the spirit, and fiction gets the material. Modern lyric poetry is assigned to track the fate of the inner life, while fiction is stuck with consciousness and material objects, neither of which speaks to the other. The stages of this process are all outlined by the Spanish philosopher Ortega y Gasset in his wonderful *Meditations on Quixote*. Don Quixote, he says, is the spirit of epic poetry who hears all things speaking; Sancho Panza is the practical materialist, the spirit of the rise of the novel. Cervantes's novel is the thunderous and comic announcement that Don Quixote is about to be supplanted in human history by Sancho Panza. Poetry, displaced by prose, can keep its heroism and its madness, but prose will be delegated to speak about material life. Poetry gets the spirit and hears it speak but is called mad; prose fiction is given a landscape of dead objects and is rewarded for writing about these things with a popular acclaim, a mass audience.

In any case, following this model, one can understand why, when Don Quixote is dying and has regained his lucidity, Sancho Panza wants him to be his old self again – heroic and mad and epical. Sancho is going to be stuck with a paunch and a world of mute things. So much the worse for him, but he *has* survived, in the way that laboratory science has survived its unruly parent, alchemy, and for some of the same reasons. Marxism survives Hegelianism until something turns up to displace dialectical materialism. Everyone remembers Sancho Panza's tears at the deathbed of Don Quixote. Materialism without ideals, mad or not, weeps. Deprived of a quest, it is consigned to centuries of weeping. Don Quixote and Sancho together are the two parts of a whole that speaks beautifully and memorably and comically. Separated, they die in different ways.

An interlude: during a particularly harsh period in my life, I was living in a rented room in Buffalo, New York. At the time, I was trying to convince myself that I loved someone I did not really love. All my emotions seemed willful and tired, like a muscle that has been overtrained. The city of Buffalo seemed to me a visual representation of the futility of all human endeavor. Like many people in my condition, I was broke all the time but did not care. Money was for others. At least, I thought, I have my cigarettes and books and enough food to live on. From day to day my personality was probably insufferable. One way or another my friends suffered it.

I had a new idea, it seemed, every five minutes. When friends came to Buffalo, I gave them a tour of the cemetery, which was, to be fair, a local attraction. I woke up at night hearing serious accusations against my life and would read D. H. Lawrence or Hegel until sunrise. I tried to silence these accusations by reading voices of massive explanation, the masters of intellectual volume. The only ideas that seemed worthy to me were those that were desperate or excessive. All my ideas about sex were inflamed. Sexually, I wanted to be a laboratory animal.

We are talking now about the psychology of private obsession, rented rooms, student life, high unsupported intellectuality, balconies with a good view that are attached to no building. It is a mode of existence that interested Dostoyevsky. In our own time Don DeLillo has written about it. Somehow I cannot think about this kind of life without seeing cigarettes and smoke and drugs as part of it, as if Faust and the dark powers must always be invoked. I do not know how I knew that thinking-at-the-frontiers required cigarettes. I just knew smoke figured into it.

One night, coming back to my rented room at about three in the morning after a particularly excruciating romantic encounter, I turned on the light in my room and saw the chair I usually sat in. This chair had high padded arms and was upholstered in what I remember as worn pale-green polyester fabric, very much in the taste of my landlady, Mrs. Zachman. I looked at the chair and the desk and the bed, and I began weeping as one weeps under such circumstances. The content of my thought was both alcoholic and sentimental. Nevertheless, my fit had a particular content.

It was Sancho Panza trying to cross over into Don Quixote, and it had to do with the belief that things would take care of me. These things, the chair and the desk, would hold me and carry me at those times when humans would not.

People in a traumatized state tend to love their furniture. They become ferociously attached to knickknacks. Laura and her love for her glass menagerie in Tennessee Williams's play will have to stand for a whole platoon of the dispossessed for whom objects have come alive. To write about these spiritual conditions, an author might do better to describe the furniture than to describe the consciousness of the person entering the room. The things carry the burden of the feeling. They do not when our emotions are placid, but when our emotions are violent, they must.

In an age of violent emotions, objects become as expressive as the people who live among them. Anglo-American fiction, unlike poetry, has been slow to arrive at this recognition. It wants to contain objects and material but to give all the feelings to the human characters. The resulting effect of articulated will and passion in the void of pure consciousness is one of the great modes of modernist fiction. The rise of delineated consciousness in fiction, powerful and solitary as it grasps for a handle on the world, is so apparent in the twentieth century that it needs no further elaboration from me. My intention in the remainder of this essay is to single out certain passages of fiction that I love, where objects rather than people are expressive or even sentient. Behind these moments I hear John Ruskin clearing his throat, but I think that Ruskin's clarity of categories operates best in moments of nonviolence free of atrocity. For this and other reasons I think of the pathetic fallacy not so much as a dated concept but as a critical urban pastoral.

For years, each time I read the "Time Passes" section of *To the Lighthouse*, it puzzled me. These twenty-four pages of Virginia Woolf's prose struck me at one time as somehow both fey and bizarre. I understood – I was a graduate student – how Woolf wanted to reincorporate material objects in fiction with what she called a "luminous halo" and how her quarrel with the novels of Arnold Bennett had to do with the manner in which objects appeared in fiction. She concluded that Bennett was a crude materialist and that this produced in his novels an offensive knowingness about worldly things. What she wanted, by contrast, was the spiritualization of the world of objects.

All the same, "Time Passes" looked odd no matter how I read it. The sheer writerly heroism of the section, its courage, eluded me. With the snobbery of middle age, I now believe that an understanding of this rather singular interlude is aided by a reader's experience of or feeling for immediate – even personal – decay. Having gotten over being young is an aid in reading it.

The main character in the section is the Ramsay house, vacated by the Ramsays, as it gradually loses its integrity and form. The other two actors are darkness and wind. Human beings are, in this section, secondary to objects and spirits. There is a cleaning woman, Mrs. McNab, and her helper, Mrs. Bast, both of whom appear late in the section to clean things up, but when the members of the Ramsay family are mentioned, their names and their actions appear within brackets.

Death, often violent or sudden, is held within these brackets: Mrs. Ramsay's sudden death from an unnamed illness; Prue Ramsay's death in childbirth; Andrew Ramsay's death in the First World War. These calamities are narrated with a shocking offhandedness. The narrative consciousness of *To the Lighthouse* refuses to dwell on them. They are the stuff of trauma, and in the world of this novel they are in some fundamental sense nonnarratable. Beyond stating the bare facts, trauma declines to speak of itself. The odd purity of true suffering, in this case, is that it is resolutely undemonstrative; unless our sensibilities are corrupt, the facts must always be the sufficient shock. Any narrative inflation of pain is an exploitation of it and a betrayal of its nature. In this novel the death of the spirit cannot be housed narratively in the flesh where that death occurs but must move into the dwelling place of the body, the house itself.

What happens in this section tonally has a touch of fable, horror movie, and children's story. In passages such as the following I hear a voice almost unknown to the modernist novel:

Only through the rusty hinges and swollen sea-moistened woodwork certain airs, detached from the body of the wind (the house was ramshackle after all) crept round corners and ventured indoors. Almost one might imagine them, as they entered the drawing-room questioning and wondering, toying with the flap of hanging wall-paper, asking, would it hang much longer, when would it fall?

I recognize this voice. It says, "Now listen, children." At some outer limit of pain, innocence is being allowed to enter through a back door, a secret entrance. Abstract qualities are given human form at the same time that humans lose it.

> Loveliness and stillness clasped hands in the bedroom, and among the shrouded jugs and sheeted chairs even the prying of the wind, and the soft nose of the clammy sea airs, rubbing, snuffling, iterating, and reiterating their questions – "Will you fade? Will you perish?" – scarcely disturbed the peace, the indifference, the air of pure integrity, as if the question they asked scarcely needed that they should answer: we remain.

As the members of the family die, the house is invaded by wind and rain and darkness. We are witnessing the soul of a house as it expires. The feeling in these passages is wonderfully and beautifully peculiar. As saucepans rust, the mats decay, and the toads invade the interior, and as the lighthouse watches "with equanimity" while the house is undermined, all forms of the pathetic fallacy are put on display. But, if I can put it this way, what is being projected onto the house is not a human feeling, but a god's. Spirits give life, but in this case they also rot. The tone of the sentences mixes wonderment and incantation; it is a tone I am familiar with from children's literature, but the English novel does not to my knowledge display it with high seriousness until this moment. This leap-to-childhood does not feel regressive to me so much as desperate and enterprising. Some ancient source of wonder has to be traced back to its origin if life is to be sustained at all. If humans are to suffer spirit-death, things will too. By this means the "something" that lies behind our objects will be glimpsed.

> But there was a force working; something not highly conscious; something that leered, something that lurched; something not inspired to go about its work with dignified ritual or solemn chanting.

This "something" has to be tricked out of hiding. Solemn chanting will not do the trick, but (at the level of style) fable, lyric, whimsy, lushness just might. The "something" spied in this passage is not malign; but it does not gaze with equanimity either, as the lighthouse does. It is a dead god being brought back to life in the revival of things in which it can find habitation. As the house is restored, so is the presence that lies behind it.

For any number of reasons, I find this section of *To the Lighthouse* wildly, almost insanely, courageous. In a voice invoking magic, it equates housekeeping with religion. It says that taking care of things, both natural and man-made, is the way back to the reconstitution of the spirit, and it gives a sentience to objects as the containers of that spirit. It declares a truce between humans and objects, and it observes that if any group effects the repair, it will probably be women, women who have never read Descartes, who would not understand Descartes if they did read him. Against the absolute separation of man and thing, the mind-body dichotomy tormenting Mr. Ramsay, we just might place a therapeutic incomprehension. "One wanted," Lily Briscoe thinks, "to be on a level with ordinary experience. . . ."

The solemn and lyrical zaniness of "Time Passes," its cast of characters of rats, frogs, wind, darkness, and spirit, makes it immune, I think, to skepticism and epistemological badgering. The person who asks, "How do you *know* that loveliness and stillness clasped hands in the bedroom?" is immediately recognizable as a fool; the question is absurd in a way that the assertion of the clasped hands is not.

In *To the Lighthouse* the reconciliation of matter and spirit is managed at such a high level of psychic virtuosity that one holds one's breath while reading it. Aesthetically, it almost does not happen, in the same way that James Ramsay is almost not reconciled to his father as they sail out to the lighthouse in the closing pages of the book. James wants to kill his father, knife him for his emotional coldness and his other crimes against the spirit. But the winds fill the sails at the last moment, Mr. Ramsay says, "Well done!" and James "was so pleased that he was not going to let anyone share a grain of his pleasure." Opportunistic violence is bracketed at last and removed from the scene of narrative.

The fragility of these narrative instances can hardly be overstated. I do not find anything much like it, certainly in American writing, for another two decades. What happens instead is a narrative interest in the anger of objects, the fierce hostility of things to man and his enterprises. A few examples will have to stand for what I take to be a larger field of activity.

Here is Malcolm Lowry's consul in *Under the Volcano,* sitting in a bath-room, drunk, and gazing at the insects on the wall:

The Consul sat helplessly in the bathroom, watching the insects which lay at dif-ferent angles from one another on the wall, like ships out on the roadstead. A caterpillar started to wriggle toward him, peering this way and that, with interroga-tory antennae. A large cricket, with polished fuselage, clung to the curtain, sway-ing it slightly and cleaning its face like a cat, its eyes on stalks appearing to revolve in its head. . . . Now a scorpion was moving slowly across towards him. Suddenly the Consul rose, trembling in every limb. But it wasn't the scorpion he cared about. It was that, all at once, the thin shadows of isolated nails, the stains of mur-dered mosquitoes, the very scars and cracks of the wall, had begun to swarm, so that, wherever he looked, another insect was born, wriggling instantly toward his heart. It was as if, and this was what was most appalling, the whole insect world had somehow moved nearer and now was closing, rushing in upon him.

The consul expresses insects. Having been expressed, they return to him, to their insect home, his heart. They are grotesque, of course, not only because they are hideous but also and especially because they hate him. He is defined – he defines himself – as a character who refuses to love. Therefore he gets the insects. They are like tiny violence-prone fates.

Thomas Pynchon's Byron the Light Bulb (in *Gravity's Rainbow*) trav-els from bulb babyhood to a tour of the world's systemic cartels, including the light cartel, Phoebus. In Pynchon's encapsulated light-bulb *bildungs-roman*, Byron, who is immortal, sees the truth of the human systems but "is condemned to go on forever, knowing the truth and powerless to change anything. No longer will he seek to get off the wheel. His anger and frustration will grow without limit, and he will find himself, poor per-verse bulb, enjoying it. . . ."

As in much of Pynchon, this Olympian understanding leads to an im-mobilized rage. It is now power rather than capital that moves in a tidal ebb and flow, and – in a very Foucaultian manner – one's understanding of the system is essentially paralytic. Anger and frustration expand to fill any space available to house them.

Another way of saying this is to argue that the speech and the feelings traded between human beings and objects, both animate and inanimate, have something to do with a contract. The contract's language is not always easy to decipher; nevertheless, it concerns how humans will employ the things that come to hand. In what I can make out of this contract, as it becomes visible in twentieth-century fiction, the earth is described (in a traditional metaphor) as a home. When greed, violence, and the various other human vices begin to make the home unhomelike – in German, *un-heimlich* – the uncanny erupts out of things that were once silent. Objects are forced to speak, to become visible as thoughtful, when the home is endangered. The double meaning of *unheimlich* as both *unhomelike* and *uncanny* is a traditional puzzle. Freud worried over it in his "On the Uncanny" and saw it, in part, as the estrangement of the familiar. We might describe the uncanny here as "the speaking or thinking of mute, thoughtless things."

Certainly it arises, as Ruskin predicted it would, from emotional violence and extremity. The examples I have cited so far all have warfare – the First World War, the Spanish Civil War, and the Second World War – deeply painted in the background. In some cases, again in fiction, where warfare or imperialism are not explicitly implied, the hidden subject may be described as soul-theft. This tradition is very strong in Russian literature and finds its great artist in Nikolai Gogol, whose work tracks and shadows the soul as it is bought and sold, and in whose work objects seem to be living a giddy life of their own. Leo Tolstoy, too: in the first section of "The Death of Ivan Ilych," Pavel Ivanovich suffers the pranksterish rebellious springs of the chair he sits on, while Praskovya Fedorovna, the grieving widow, gets her shawl stuck on the side of a table. These are not accidents; the objects want it that way. Loveless, petty functionaries, in Tolstoy's account, come face to face with the perversity of inanimate objects, beginning with their sickening bodies and going on from there. The trading and buying of souls enlivens the uncanny in Andrei Bely, Mikhail Bulgakov, and Vladimir Nabokov as well; in Nabokov's *Bend Sinister*, located in a police state where the dictator Paduk is doing his best to acquire the soul of the philosopher Adam Krug, Krug's friends, the little things, haplessly sing tunes to him he can only half-see and half-hear.

The stove crackled gently, and a square clock with two cornflowers painted on its white wooden face and no glass rapped out the seconds in pica type. The window attempted a smile. A faint infusion of sunshine spread over the distant hill and brought out with a kind of pointless distinction the little farm and three pine trees on the opposite slope which seemed to move forward and then to retreat again as the wan sun swooned.

If this is the pathetic fallacy, whose pathos is it? The internal narrator's? Krug's? Nabokov's? These floating perceptions have a detachment that is so complete that they have a feeling of weightlessness, an immunity to gravity. In this sense they have the god-feeling of "Time Passes," a forthright and almost vehement innocence, the song the angels sing that cannot for all of its beauty relieve the torments of human life.

Perhaps such innocence must be brought out by dualities, by an opposition of brutality or violence. I began this essay by arguing that objects can speak back to us and let us know their thoughts in fiction suffused with a tone of balance and equilibrium, but I am suspicious of that claim because its best examples are not found in fiction but in poetry. It may be that the native tension of narrative fiction is more conducive to an edgy relation to things, a set of mutually accusing voices.

Still – and here I wander guilelessly into a major problem of philosophy – it is recognizable that a tree or a sidewalk café viewed by a person in love are not the same objects when viewed by a person with congestive heart failure. Conventionally we say that the tree is *viewed* differently by those two people. But it takes a third person to say so. In the kind of fiction I have been discussing here, it is not a matter of the tree being viewed differently. The tree itself is different.

The word "setting," especially as it is used in fiction-writing textbooks and workshops, has a drab, dutiful quality, a feeling of something always already-there. Worse, it may be assumed that setting is objective, that it "helps" or "shapes" a story. In the way that I am describing them, however, the objects and things surrounding fictional characters have the same status as the characters themselves, and an equal portion of energy. Setting, then, is *not* just a place where action occurs, any more than the earth is a prized location where our lives happen to happen. Setting in its psychic extensiveness projects a mode of feeling that corresponds to, or contrasts with, the action. The way that setting is usually taught in fiction-writing classes results in the fictional equivalent of a curtain that rises on a stage set with one desk, one potted plant, and a stairway reaching toward empty air. What surrounds the characters can be and often should be as expressive as the action, but no law or formal entitlement dictates that it should always express the feelings of the characters. Too often, however, it does. Let us call this the fallacy of the objective correlative. In the fallacy of the objective correlative, the setting can *only* express the feelings of the characters. A sad man sees sad trees. A murderer gazes upon a murderous lake.

This kind of one-to-one equivalency makes John Ruskin's ideas about the pathetic fallacy seem sensible all over again. If objects reflect *only* the characters who look upon them, they have nothing to tell us. In such cases, they function as mirrors serving to enlarge – once again – the human realm. But if there is a feeling characteristic of our time, it is that the human realm needs no further enlargement; it is already bloated, in many senses at once. If a mountain exists only to express human feeling, it is no longer itself – dangerous, unknowably beautiful, and absolutely nonhuman. Malcolm Lowry's consul does see versions of himself wherever he looks, but Lowry himself is careful to include other points of view in the novel to readjust the perspective and to let other versions of nature speak. Lowry does not let his character dictate the terms of the novel's telling. The consul's presence makes *Under the Volcano* possible, but the novel also requires his absence from time to time. I think it also requires his death, or at least his sacrifice; he is a character who must die, or at least be thrown away, so that the novel *about* and around him can live.

Is there such a condition as an expressive background of speaking objects that are heard by a reader but not by the characters themselves? Virginia Woolf points us in this direction, as does Nabokov, but in contemporary American fiction few examples suggest themselves. We are too often in the presence of characters and narrators who dictate the terms under which things, or the world itself, may speak. More often, things are not allowed to speak at all; they are every bit as inarticulate as the characters who acquire and despise them.

Examples of the mute object, broken on the thematic wheel, are so common that they do not command much attention, but objects that speak over the heads of characters directly to readers are so uncommon in fiction that the prevalence of this form of knowing and saying in the work of William Maxwell deserves some notice. Modesty and a variety of innocence that is never naive replace the usual forms of worldliness and willfulness in this fiction, which is often stuck in the Midwest and stuck, too, at a particular time, the 1920s and '30s. Its rather astonishing love for its characters – astonishing only for its size and generosity – may be a function of its nostalgia, but in this case nostalgia acts as a perpetual questioning of what constituted the place that a person could once call "home." It is probably consistent with this questioning that most of Maxwell's characters are fated to fall in love with the wrong thing or the wrong person. They experience love just long enough to know what love is; then the object of that love, being wrong, is removed. (In this respect his work bears a single, odd resemblance to that of Toni Morrison.)

In Maxwell's *Time Will Darken It*, Nora Potter, the young woman who will fall in love with a married man, Austin King, is located at the center of what would be in other respects a conventional narrative – if the town where it occurs, Draperville, Illinois, were not so articulate. But in this novel, because everything is loved, everything speaks. The "mindless, kindless voice of nature," as the narrator calls it, speaks through the heat, the locusts, the rain, and the bric-a-brac. Spoken only to the reader, it bypasses the characters. One example from many will have to suffice.

> The house was so still that it gave her the feeling that she was being watched, that the sofas and chairs were keeping an eye on her to see that she didn't touch anything that she shouldn't; that she put back the alabaster model of the Taj Mahal and the little bearded grinning man (made out of ivory, with a pack on his back, a folded fan, and his toes turned inward) exactly the way she found them. The locusts warned her, but from too far away. The clocks all seemed preoccupied with their various and contradictory versions of the correct time.

This passage begins with Nora's feelings, but it has more feelings than Nora does, and by the time the paragraph is over, Nora is insufficient to explain them. She has been diminished just enough so that the locusts can speak without being heard by her. The passage notices that the little bearded man made out of ivory has toes turned inward, but it is unclear whether Nora notices that. Here, she is one thing in a field of things. And she is about to violate those things, without being quite aware that she is doing so. If we have caught the feeling of the scene, we probably know that Nora is going to suffer eventually, that things (in this case, in the form of fire) will have their revenge for her interference.

In this tender, antiheroic fiction, Maxwell lovingly puts his characters

in their places; like Turgenev's Lavretsky and like Chekhov's characters, they slowly learn what it means to have a sense of scale. In the only
way that matters, they are humbled by being placed in proximity to objects that, in Turgenev's words, seem to know where they are going.

In two other contemporary stories, objects acquire humaneness when
humans themselves cannot possess it. In Cynthia Ozick's "The Shawl,"
a story about a concentration camp, the shawl takes on the burden of nur-
turing Magda, a malnourished infant, and becomes a breast and a womb
and a house. The electric fencing around the death camp, as if disturbed
by the role it plays, hums with "grainy sad voices." In Tim O'Brien's *The
Things They Carried*, about Vietnam, the soldiers transfer all their feelings
to the objects they "hump," as the narrative has it: feeling, dispossessed
by humans, moves quickly into the nearest receptacle willing to house it.

A final interlude (or a postlude): My stepfather liked on winter weekends
to repair broken furniture, and he often gave me the responsibility of
holding his tools while he did the work. Because he was a man of small
patience and a terrible temper, but with a high vision of himself, he
would turn screws or hammer nails with a bland expression on his face
that revealed almost nothing. Only his skin revealed his feelings: it grew
redder and redder as his fury against inanimate objects increased. Holding his tools, I thought: He is a steam engine, and he is going to explode
any minute now.

He never cursed and hardly spoke while doing these tasks. He took
himself as an upper-class, lapsed Protestant very seriously. But when he
exhaled, he exhaled through his nose in regular three-second intervals,
exhalations of the purest rage, utterly machinelike, so much so that I cannot now hear the distant sound of a stamping plant or a production line
without thinking of my stepfather. Holding his tools, I felt sorry for the
screws and the nails. They screamed and squeaked as they fell under my
stepfather's interest.

Outside my window is an apple tree. It is August as I write these sentences. For the last few days a squirrel has been foraging in the tree, and
sometimes it descends low enough on one of the branches in front of my
study window to take a good look at me. It can stare at me for two minutes
without moving. Then it goes back to its business, as I do to mine.

We do not spray the tree, and the apples growing there are mostly green or wormy. During the time that I have been writing this essay, the apples have been falling to the ground in the backyard. Every now and then, writing a sentence, I have heard the sound of an apple hitting the earth. Before the sound of that impact, there is a breath, a swish, as the fruit drops through the branches and leaves. It is not a sigh but sounds like one. This sound has nothing to do with my current moods, but I listen for it, and I have been counting the number of apples that have fallen during the last ten pages of this essay. There have been eighteen.

DAVID WOJAHN AND LYNDA HULL

Mercantile Eyes:
Travel Poems and Tourist Poems

[INDIANA UNIVERSITY WRITERS' CONFERENCE]

The following lecture was written collaboratively: discussions of poems by
Adam Zagajewski and Elizabeth Bishop, the film by Wim Wenders, the introduction, and half the conclusion were contributed by Lynda Hull; the discussion of
Mary Jo Salter's poem, Michael Blumenthal's poem, and half the conclusion were
written by David Wojahn. The lecture was delivered by both authors, each reading the sections they had penned.

Let me offer you a few snapshots from my travels that comment metaphorically on my subject, the situation that confronts the American poet
when he or she voyages into foreign cultures. First, let me show you the
Gran Via in Madrid, stretching graciously from a fountain showing Nep-
tune rising triumphant in his carriage from the sea, meant to commemo-
rate Spain's mastery over the sea routes, toward the imperial complex;
it's a royal parade route in a city built as a capital for the Castilian kings.
Today its swarming Baroque buildings are blackened from Madrid's endless clamor of traffic, and soot-faced cherubim frolic over tacky flamenco
palaces and restaurants posting *menus turisticas.* Palazzos transformed to
movie palaces trumpet the latest Hollywood schmaltz – *Police Academy
III, A Nightmare on Elm Street, Troop Beverly Hills.* Gran Via is also graced
by the world's most elegant McDonald's, a building that once housed
one of the nation's largest banks. A marble and brass interior swooping
with balconies houses the familiar counter and menu board offering Big
Macs and McPollo sandwiches. These are not a conqueror's grand monuments, but vividly and uncomfortably illustrate the Americanization

that's occurred in Spain at an accelerated rate since Franco's death.

Another scene: Plock, a small city northwest of Warsaw where, last fall, my mother was reunited with the remnants of her family. We are sitting in a small, sparsely furnished room overflowing with people weeping and embracing, and through the lavish shush and murmur of Polish I can hear a familiar theme song. On a small black-and-white a waterfall flickers and opening credits roll. It's *Twin Peaks*, David Lynch's violent and surreally American foray into TV drama. The episode is badly dubbed so that the English is still audible a second before the Polish – more like one of those U.N. simultaneous translations. Amidst bitter talk of the Soviet regime, we learn that one of my cousins has just been hired on at the new Levi Strauss plant in town. The Poles are very ambivalent about the inroads these American imports are already making in their country, and so am I, the American traveler nibbling at the hand-picked mushrooms placed before us, sipping the home-pressed cherry juice. Earlier that day we'd eaten a restaurant meal that would have cost the average Pole a month's wages.

Once again, I found myself reminded that this is our century, as the nineteenth century was for the British. Beginning in the late 1700s and early 1800s, the concept of the grand tour was initiated. With British power in the ascendancy, flocks of tourists crossed the Channel to travel the Continent, and beyond to even more exotic places. Think of those crass or hapless or moonstruck Victorians (familiar from Merchant Ivory films) laden with trunks, guidebooks and a passel of misapprehensions, all of it seasoned with a dose of xenophobia. The aim of these tourists, even those traveling under the aegis of "science," was essentially encyclopedic – the accumulation of souvenirs, charming experiences, sketches, plunder, knowledge, cultural artifacts. (One has only to visit the Victoria and Albert or the British Museum to get the point.) I'm talking about a form of colonialism, or exploitation. Among the tourist flocks we also see literary voyagers – the likes of Shelley, Byron, Coleridge, and the young Wordsworth, for whom travel mapped an inner journey as well as a passionate engagement with foreign landscapes. In a broad sense, then, one might draw a distinction between the *tourist*, whose impulse is largely acquisitive, that of the consumer and bystander, and the *traveler*, whose impulse is to witness, a standpoint perhaps more receptive, more self-questioning, more ambivalent and ironic. A traveler's viewpoint, then, might be called more poetic in the sense that it is about the process of discovery and is transformative. Travel can give us back to ourselves different, changed in the way that the speaker of Rilke's "Archaic Torso of Apollo" so urgently admonishes.

I don't mean to be crudely reductive or to establish easy dichotomies. All of us have been tourists and travelers by turns. Shelley himself, the anarchistic anti-imperialist, could whine and behave with imperious patronization toward the Italians among whom he exiled himself. Nor do I mean to be simplistic about the act of traveling, which is a complex and laden experience. The root of travel, as William Matthews reminds us, is *travail*, work. Complex things set us voyaging: curiosity, the need for change, escapism, the impulse to exile, the urge to find new perspectives, or a longing that is almost erotic – the desire for the experience of otherness. We are seeking here, though, to examine not behavior but vision realized through writing and to look at the pitfalls and risks attendant in writing about foreign places and people, to isolate strategies that seem useful in making the successful poem of travel.

In this century we have become heirs to the tradition of the writerly grand tour. Particularly since World War II, American artists have swarmed abroad in unprecedented numbers and their "thematic colonization" of the rest of the world has been abundantly evident. Part of this results from an increase in grant and fellowship money, a benefit of postwar affluence. Guggenheim Fellowships have been available since the twenties, but beginning in the fifties awards such as the Prix de Rome, the Amy Lowell Fellowship (which stipulates the recipient engage in foreign travel), and Fulbright and NEA fellowships have afforded writers the chance to "widen their horizons."

Elizabeth Bishop, Robert Lowell, James Wright, Richard Howard, Anthony Hecht, Adrienne Rich, W. S. Merwin, Richard Wilbur, and John Ashbery, along with many other lesser lights, all spent time abroad in the fifties and naturally the poems spun out, some distinguished, many more not. This era heralded a plethora of bad, merely shallow "Roman fountain" poems. Here's Henry James commenting on the seduction of the flimsily rendered exotic: "Our observation of any foreign land is extremely superficial." Auden writing on the difficulty of travel as a subject notes the manner in which it "restricts freedom of invention while [offering] the lure of journalism, of superficial typewriter-thumping." Many of these poems were written, as Robert Von Hallberg notes in *American Poetry and Culture*, by writers "simply glad for the chance to write descriptive poetry," as were poems impelled by a vague social impulse, hence a number of character sketches, typically focusing on stereotypical European "virtues."

Unconsciously or not, Americans were powered by an urge, according to Von Hallberg, to "assume the custodianship of European cultural traditions as militarily and economically the U.S. had taken responsibility for the postwar recovery." The issue arose as early as 1944 when Eisenhower warned his military commanders to "move cautiously around the monuments and cultural centers which symbolize to the world all that we are fighting to preserve." So we see in these travel poems, and in the poems that continue to be written, the old proprietary stance: poem after poem is an act of appropriation, and as Von Hallberg comments, some of the poets could not help but see Europe figuratively as a museum with themselves as custodians. Writers establish their authority over their subjects in a variety of ways, among them "reading" monuments and experiences "for analogies to the moral life of the individual" – parables, in essence – or, as currently fashionable jargon would have it, reading them as "texts." Another favored stance is for the speaker to exempt him- or herself from mere touristhood, to assume that the American poet abroad is somehow above the run-of-the-mill, often in fact more fit than the natives to appreciate the surrounding bounty, typically speaking *for* rather than speaking *about* the subject. This pitfall runs through the whole English and American tradition of travel poems. Edward Said in his book *Orientalism* speaks about this kind of imperialism in regard to early Mideastern scholars whose "inauguration of orientalism . . . established the figure of the Orientalist as a central authority *for* the Orient, [and] . . . put into cultural circulation a form of discursive currency by whose presence henceforth the Orient would be *spoken for*."

Of course many writers from the fifties onward sensed this connection between tourism and imperialism and the best poems admit uncertainty, admit that "empires run on rapine, and poets follow empires – the plunder sometimes being imaginative" (Von Hallberg, p. 80). Think, for instance, of Bishop's superb collection *Questions of Travel*, in which the poet herself is implicated in the appropriation of Brazil along with the conquistadors she evokes in "Brazil, January 1, 1502." Both Bishop and Lowell, in Von Hallberg's assessment, "wrote with a sense of imperial doom" during the optimistic fifties, an awareness all of us most likely hold in our own troubled present. Also, "American poets are usually aware, painfully so, of being the unacknowledged representatives of national culture, of vulgarity, wealth, and power, and implicated in the expansion of empire": hence my complicated sense of shame, guilt, and anger at the panorama of the Gran Via or the encounter in my Polish cousin's sitting room.

In Poland, that country where the most savage events of modern times transpired, I was acutely aware that the United States was a major player in all three of the century's most pivotal historical events: World Wars I and II, and the development of the bomb. Furthermore, one might venture that the United States has profited economically from these cataclysms while remaining relatively unscathed, and has emerged as a culture with the means of spreading influence across the globe. So, in essence the victims of history have been anybody but Americans. The poet-traveler abroad cannot escape the vivid evidence of our insidious presence, our influence in even very remote areas or those newly open to the "West." It seems, then, that this awareness is part of the baggage we carry along with our blue jeans and toothpaste.

Perhaps some of the best commentary on this has come from non-American artists. In *Kings of the Road,* Wim Wenders's searing satire of a road movie, two young Germans – an itinerant projector repairman and the hitchhiker he picks up – travel through West Germany in a massive American-built RV. The odyssey becomes a search for the hitchhiker's past, an ultimately frustrated journey of reconciliation, retrieval, and forgiveness. The two end up at an abandoned East German border post that the hitchhiker recalls from a youthful weekend: it is the place he first made love. Slashed all over the walls is Yank graffiti, territorial marks of American presence. The hitchhiker says, "Now the Americans have everything." In essence, the vandalism is the appropriation of more than a place, an emblem, but of memory, the past. It's a perfect act by a mass culture that all too often seems hell-bent on a kind of endless and oblivious self-erasure as well as a gratuitous assertion of its continuing power.

Earlier I mentioned that travel can give the traveler back to him- or herself changed. I'd like now to let the Polish poet Adam Zagajewski conjure a night in America from the point of view of the foreigner. A universal experience of all tourist/travelers is alienation, a vertiginous response to the strangeness, the otherness, of the visited place that causes heightened perception and intensity of vision, but also a phantasmagorical dislocation. The self, too, becomes other. "Watching *Shoah* in a Hotel Room in America" is set in that most impersonal of places, an American hotel room.

There are nights as soft as fur on a foal
but we prefer chess or card playing. Here,
some hotel guests sing "Happy Birthday"
as the one-eyed TV nonchalantly shuffles its images.
The trees of my childhood have crossed an ocean
to greet me coolly from the screen.
Polish peasants engage with a Jesuitical zest
in theological disputes: only the Jews are silent,
exhausted by their long dying.
The rivers of the voyages of my youth flow
cautiously over the distant, unfamiliar continent.
Hay wagons haul not hay, but hair,
their axles squeaking under the feathery weight.
We are innocent, the pines claim.
The SS officers are haggard and old,
doctors struggle to save them their hearts, lives, consciences.
It's late, the insinuations of drowsiness have me.
I'd sleep but my neighbors
choir "Happy Birthday" still louder:
louder than the dying Jews.
Huge trucks transport stars from the firmament,
gloomy trains go by in the rain.
I am innocent, Mozart repents;
only the aspen, as usual, trembles,
prepared to confess all its crimes.
The Czech Jews sing the national anthem: "Where is my home . . ."
There is no home, houses burn, the cold gas whistles within.
I grow more innocent, sleepy.
The TV reassures me: both of us
are beyond suspicion.
The birthday is noisier.
The shoes of Auschwitz, in pyramids

high as the sky, groan faintly:
Alas, we outlived mankind, now
let us sleep, sleep:
we have nowhere to go.

It's a shattering poem, and much of its relentless force issues from its
ironic restraint, from the strategies the poet uses to create a sense of alien-
ated dislocation. Everything arrives mediated. The "one-eyed TV nonchalantly shuffles its images," a chilling description of the medium's
monstrous mechanical dispassion as it flickers Claude Lanzmann's epic
documentary on the Holocaust. The Americans' singing of "Happy
Birthday" is filtered through the wall; all are distanced from the "[night]
soft as fur on a foal" outside the hotel. Zagajewski makes skillful use of
personification throughout to increase the poem's phantasmagorical
quality, its fluid sense of historical time and reality. The televised images
fuse with the poet's memories of his native country and become disturbingly animate: "the trees of my childhood have crossed an ocean / to greet
me coolly from the screen." Later, "the pines," "the aspen," and "the
shoes of Auschwitz," through an unsettling displacement, introduce the
key terms of the poem's argument: the issues of culpability and what constitutes humanity. The poet makes powerful use of the idea of silence:
those "Polish peasants engage with . . . zest / in theological disputes,"
but the victims, the Jews, "are silent," a reverberant absence. In travel
one turns in on one's past, one's memories: as the speaker watches *Shoah*,
the Polish scenes collide with the blank Americanscape and those oblivious singers to create a palimpsest.

Through ironic undercutting of lyricism with savage imagery, Zagajewski interrogates the concept of "innocence." Look again at this violated pastoral passage: "The rivers . . . of my youth / cautiously flow over
the distant, unfamiliar continent. / Hay wagons haul not hay, but hair, /
their axles squeaking under the feathery weight." Auschwitz, which has
been preserved as an eloquent museum, is thirty miles away from Kra-
kow, where the poet grew up. Those "haggard and old" SS officers,
attempting in the film to salve their "consciences," had stored in ware-
houses mountains of hair and clothes and shoes. In great bins at the camp
one can still see this. There are rows of poplar and aspen at the perimeter

of the camp, that were planted by prisoners, that were to screen what was going on inside.

This poem reenacts in microcosm how the world chose ignorance, chose to screen itself from the realities of the Final Solution. Those "innocent" Americans foolishly celebrating, the "innocent" speaker, even Mozart, the paradigm of Austrian artistic achievement – all deny culpability. "The TV reassures me: both of us / are beyond suspicion." His descent into sleep occurs while the Jews ask "Where is my home," while "the cold gas whistles," disturbingly echoing the victims' poisonous passage into terminal sleep. Through the poet's use of "innocence," he ironically explores guilt. We know that his sleep will be one burdened by the tortured dream of history. It is those "shoes of Auschwitz" that "groan faintly" the last word, a statement that poses a question; if they have "outlived mankind," what kind of humanity *is* left? Where does one go after such knowledge? In this poem of travel, then, through the use of irony, ambiguity, and self-confrontation, everyone is implicated.

To again quote Von Hallberg, Zagajewski has indeed "read" experience "for analogies to the moral life of the individual." But even within the grimly anesthetizing abstraction of the Holocaust as seen on a hotel TV screen, Zagajewski seeks to reaffirm a sense of the most abject horror, a horror that is finally resistant to the forces that seek to abstract it. The Holocaust, he reminds us, is not merely another text; it cannot be deconstructed. Perhaps one of the reasons why Zagajewski's poem is so effective is that it claims no implicit control of its subjects, nor even anything more than a very provisional understanding of them; the speaker can no more turn off the chorus of drunken revelers singing "Happy Birthday" than he can turn away from the grisly footage of the Auschwitz warehouse of victims' shoes. Zagajewski, born in 1945, is not himself a Holocaust survivor, yet his poem is informed by a complex sense of history, both personal and public, that is perhaps unavailable to most of his American contemporaries.

How *is* travel treated by current American poets? *The Morrow Anthology of Younger American Poets* offers a partial but somewhat distressing answer. The 105 figures it represents, all born between 1940 and 1955, are Zagajewski's contemporaries, and to judge from the selections they do a lot of traveling. Twenty-eight of the poets have among their selections poems that have foreign settings or that discuss foreign travel. Predictably, they favor Italy and France over most other locales, as a sampling of some of the poems' openings suggests: "A hot, bright day. Late June. The bus from Rome / passed a seaside town..." (Rika Lesser); "The natives [of Champagne]... have given up their backyards / and are happy where we cannot see them..." (Rita Dove); "Although you mention Venice / keeping it on your tongue like a fruit pit / and I say yes, perhaps Bucharest, neither of us / really knows..."(Carolyn Forché); "Driving, driven / the driven sun, the sun- / slicked autostrada, glare / more slippery than ice... / Genova to L'Aquila in ten hours..." (Nicholas Christopher); "... in Gubbio, an Umbrian city / the most purely medieval in Italy, the buildings..." (Daniel Halpern). It goes without saying that none of these openings is particularly promising. Halpern seems afflicted with a case of Arthur Frommer–speak, and although Dove begins by implying an intriguing contrast between the speaker and the Champagne "natives," her language is quite pedestrian. But stylistic limitations are only part of the problem. The real difficulties of the poems are embedded in what may be called their perspectives; Lesser looks out the windows of a bus; Christopher is speeding down the boot of Italy (in an Alfa Romeo, presumably); Forché is in a train compartment, having met a mysterious stranger out of Central Casting. None of this trio is *within* a landscape as much as passing through it. If travel offers us a text, these poets take the Evelyn Wood approach to reading it, and none seems to question this process.

Perhaps the inevitable consequence of such superficiality is to simplify the issues implicit in travel poetry even further. Why go overseas to exploit foreign culture when it can be more easily and cheaply written about at home? Isn't the studio backlot perfectly adequate? The *Morrow Anthology*'s selections of Michael Blumenthal's poetry contain a competently written love poem set in Assisi ("This morning, in Assisi, I woke / and looked into my wife's face / and thought of St. Francis..." he begins.) But more telling is the poem that precedes it, "Today I Am Envying the Glorious Mexicans."

The title is also its first line, and the speaker's envy becomes the subject of the twenty-two-line poem, which is written in a loose pentameter. The speaker envies the "glorious" inhabitants of Mexico who siesta beneath their sombreros beside "unambitious" cacti. He envies a pair of imagined Mexican lovers, who are awaiting a liaison in the moonlight. He envies grass, which is compared to "the green whiskers of God." His catalogue of envies eventually takes a somewhat magical realist turn – the "singing" dead and the genitalia of flowers are listed, and the poem eventually transforms itself into a kind of loopy prayer: the speaker implores the almighty to let him live a bit longer, so that he can learn to emulate his Mexicans' and flowers' lack of purpose. His goal seems to be a sort of giddy self-forgetfulness. "I want to be the perfect madman," he tells us, "without reflection," capable of "babbling" on endlessly to himself. Fortunately, the poem begins to wind down at this point and concludes with a sort of smiley-face trope – something about "sangria" and "the happy earth."

Although I am not sure that the poem achieves the speaker's goal of becoming the perfect madman, his other goal, of being "without reflection," has been consummately attained. One needn't be rabidly PC to see that the poem's view of the "glorious Mexicans" is a reprehensible stereotype – happy, indolent Panchos and Ciscos, dozing in sombreros beneath the midday sun, slugging tequila among the saguaros. True, there's a certain element of self-mockery in the poem's tone, which is complimented by the flourishes of Nerudaesque surrealism – "the singing dead," "the green whiskers of God." Yet Blumenthal's self-mockery does not extend to any sort of questioning of the stereotypes he has exploited. His envy of the Mexicans is a yuppie update of the cult of the noble savage, and it is hard to believe that such reactionary sentiments could be expressed in a poem published as recently as the mid-1980s.

Yet the poem's willingness to traffic in stereotypes is in some ways less troubling than a more subtle problem. Where, we have to ask, do the glorious Mexicans come from? Do they arise from a memory that the speaker has half-forgotten and that is now suddenly released? Is he remembering an actual visit to Mexico, or has he discovered the motif through armchair travel, from Weston's Mexican photos of the thirties, for example? Our only clue to this enigma is that we are told the envy is occurring "today." Is our speaker *in* Mexico as he writes the poem, then, back in his hotel room after having scavenged the countryside for local color? Any of these explanations is of course possible, but the most likely explanation is that the Mexicans come from none of these sources, that they were conjured by the speaker as he sought to crank out his daily quota of poem. Creative writing teachers are fond of repeating that truism that any subject is a proper one for a poem, and in many instances this claim is valid. But good poems should also incorporate into their structure some element that attempts to analyze the poet's motives for writing about a subject. Poems without this quality run the risk of treating subject matter in the way that conquistadors and Visigoths saw plunder. Blumenthal may claim to envy his glorious Mexicans, but his true allegiance is to Cortez and Pizarro.

Perhaps an important requirement for any good travel poem is that it must, even more than other sorts of poems, build a recognition of the gap between motive and subject matter into its very structure. As an impetus of self-questioning, the alienation inherent in travel is at least as strong a catalyst as are those forces which we commonly associate with self-interrogation. Travel causes us to look into ourselves just as uncomfortably as do guilt, regret, and a recognition of aging. Travel is more an act of self-reckoning than of diversion. Blumenthal and several of the other poets represented in the *Morrow Anthology* seem too preoccupied – either with getting to the trattoria in the next Umbrian town or with finishing the next poem – to acknowledge this.

But even those of us who acknowledge the complexities and self-annihilating dangers of travel often have a difficult time balancing these concerns with the seductive appeal of the exotic. A case in point is Mary Jo Salter's Lamont Prize–winning *Unfinished Painting*. Many of the poems describe a period of living in Japan, and show a true sympathy for the culture, one strong enough to overcome some of Salter's exasperating poetic mannerisms, not the least of which is a tendency to wield form and wit like a machete. Here are two regrettable quatrains that open a poem about Chernobyl: "Once upon a time / the word alone was scary / Now, quainter than this rhyme / it's the headline of a story / long yellowed in the news / The streets were hosed in Kiev / and Poles took more shampoos. / The evacuees were brave..." The poem I would like to focus upon is better than this, but its failings are ultimately more interesting than its strengths. "I Lose You for an Instant" carries a subtitle, "Guilen, China," and its opening is animated and engaging.

> The sun's at last soaking up
> the rut-puddled street, and hundreds

of age-old unoiled bicycles
together like thunder rip

over the hump of bridge.
Out of the blue, in another
military-mud-
green jeep conveying

what looks like body bags
until one spills (just rice)
or heaps of gravel (why?)
it's a mystery

nobody can unravel
tons of it from nowhere
and deposited in the most
God-forsaken spots. . . .

Despite some clumsy gestures – the bikes on the bridge compared to thunder, for example – the opening does a good job of conveying both the scene and the speaker's sense of uncertainty within it. The parentheses and asides give a kind of querulous immediacy to the descriptions, as do the short lines and incidental rhyming. Salter carries on in this fashion for a few more stanzas, and then introduces some information that considerably complicates the poem:

I'm standing on the bridge
and under the black coat
packed that I might blend
into the bleakness I expected, am

five months pregnant.
I've dragged you all the way to China
(you dragging all the bags),
because I've been afraid

our days of exhilarating frights
are drawing to an end.
I'm scared all right. . . .

The speaker's confession of impending change in the structure of her life
— of "our days of exhilarating frights / . . . drawing to an end" — now gives
way to a purer sort of vulnerability. She is alone, pregnant, and her husband's errand has lost him in a crowd that is now seen as more threatening
than picturesque. In the city's bustle she is nonchalantly ignored by the
bicycle-pedaling crowd, but this in several ways intensifies her sense of
desolation.

> ten

> minutes I've stood here
> round-eyed, roundbellied foreigner
> whom nobody seems to mind.
> It's just occurred to me

> that I have both our passports
> and you have all our money...

This is the moment of the poem's dramatic and thematic reckoning. It is
an affecting scene, rich with implication. Salter captures the traveler's simultaneous experience of alienation and wonder, contrasts the West's
sense of individualism and privacy with the East's collectivism, and creates a fair amount of narrative suspense: Will the husband return? What
will the speaker do if he is lost? The poem's resolution of these issues
promises to be exciting. Unfortunately, the rest of the poem is over-
wrought and formulaic.

> You will come back. And time
> though it promises to fill

> full the brave new world
> with gravel, will deliver us
> a daughter — as it braids another
> river from a glossy fall

> of rain, and chooses to preserve
> as lovelier than the often

painted mountains of Guilen
so steep they ought

to come to pencil-points.
High parentheses
(enclosing that lost
instant), they rise mis-

shapen in my eyes.

Salter's almost Pavlovian wittiness, which has been admirably kept in
check up to this point, now overwhelms the poem. Salter chooses to end
with an archly descriptive flourish rather than to explore the situation's
more promising implications, which she even appears to refute. The
poem's sense of immediacy is obliterated when we are told that its first
two thirds are merely a flashback, a mere aside. The poem's final paren-
thetical remark – "(enclosing that lost / instant)" – takes a device that had
earlier been used quite effectively and reduces it to a crass typographical
pun. Salter's use of the pencil conceit near the end is also revealing.
While Salter could hardly be labeled a language poet, the implicit message of the conclusion is one of language poetry's main precepts: This
poem is not about content and experience, she tells us, but about "writing."

At that richly frictional moment in "I Lose You for an Instant" when a
personal and cultural collision occurs, Salter ice-skates away, settling for
superficial knowledge of her subject rather than a deeper involvement.
Ultimately, the poem simply exploits the experience for the sake of a
dubious technical exercise, instead of mining that experience for self-
confrontation. Let's turn now to Elizabeth Bishop's "Over 2,000 Illustrations and a Complete Concordance," which confronts similar issues:
tourist experience versus a more intense, troubling, and mysterious
traveler's experience.

The poem dislocates the reader immediately by entering into a dialogue that implies a comparison: "Thus should have been our travels: /
serious, engravable." The poet then describes plates in what is probably
one of those Victorian travel books, where all the images are somewhat
romanticized, abstracted, or sanitized.

> The Seven Wonders of the World are tired
> and a touch familiar, but the other scenes,
> innumerable, though equally sad and still,
> are foreign. Often the squatting Arab,
> or group of Arabs, plotting, probably,
> against our Christian Empire,
> while one apart, with outstretched arm and hand
> points to the Tomb, the Pit, the Sepulcher.

The opening, which with light irony undercuts its playful tone with those capitalized references to Tomb, Pit, and Sepulcher, establishes the terms the poem will negotiate: that otherness infused with fear the "foreign" can engender, notions of power both sacred and secular, the facing off of East and West, and mortality. And, whereas Salter somehow turns life into "Art," Bishop questions that tidy transformation.

> Granted a page alone or a page made up
> of several scenes arranged in cattycornered rectangles
> or circles set on stippled gray,
> granted a grim lunette,
> caught in the toils of an initial letter,
> when dwelt upon, they all resolve themselves.

Perspective and resolution are possible through representation in a way perhaps impossible in actual experience. Bishop continues to sound more deeply; this is not someone whose gaze consists of snapshots from a train: "The eye drops, weighted, through the lines / the burin made, the lines that move apart / like ripples above sand, / dispersing storms, God's spreading fingerprint, / and painfully, finally, that ignite / in watery prismatic white-and-blue."

The black and white images in the travel book conjure living-color memories of actual travel – the Narrows at St. John's; St. Peter's; "Mexico," where "the dead man lay / in a blue arcade; the dead volcanoes / glistened like Easter lilies. / The jukebox went on playing 'Ay, Jalisco!'" These are a tourist's light observations: no galvanizing transformation here – those "volcanoes," although they look like "Easter lilies," are as "dead" as the man in the arcade. So, what makes this poem a traveler's poem? Like the visual sounding in the second stanza, the poet goes again for depth in what becomes an anguished self-confrontation (though, granted, Bishop insists throughout the poem on "we"). The perceiver's emotion bleeds through in her details and in her relentless questioning. The modesty of this point of view is typical of Bishop, and typically canny, reflecting that powerfully disturbing element in travel of self-erasure and uncertainty. So, while this poem may first strike the reader as more impersonal than the Salter or Blumenthal poems, it is profoundly more honest and revealing.

The tone radically changes near the end of the middle stanza, when the poet sees "what frightened [her] most of all" (here is the sole deviation from first person plural – she says "frightened me"), a desacralized tomb that is

> one of a group under a keyhole-arched stone baldaquin
> open to every wind from the pink desert.
> An open, gritty, marble trough, carved solid
> with exhortation, yellowed
> as scattered cattle-teeth;
> half-filled with dust, not even the dust
> of the poor prophet paynim who once lay there.

She undercuts this moment as if trying to back away from where she must go next: "In a smart burnoose Khadour [the guide] looked on amused." Von Hallberg in mentioning this poem notes – and this is something the fastidious Bishop would have known – that "Khadour . . . is an Islamic figure of immortality who was the protector of mariners and river travellers." But here Bishop's imagining of the death leaves him "amused" at this outsider; it's a subtle indictment of the traveler's lightness or superficiality that the poem examines, the "infant sight" of the poem's famously ambiguous last line. Here is the poem's passionately visionary closure:

> Everything only connected by "and" and "and."
> Open the book. (The gilt rubs off the edges
> of the pages and pollinates the fingertips.)
> Open the heavy book. Why couldn't we have seen
> this old Nativity while we were at it?
> – the dark ajar, the rocks breaking with light,

an undisturbed, unbreathing flame,
colorless, sparkless, freely fed on straw,
and, lulled within, a family with pets,
– and looked and looked our infant sight away.

Everything connects in a chain – images and experiences, travel, memory, death, the desire for transformation – all linked by those conjunctions, but eluding a kind of design, some ultimate fusing with the object of desire. The imperative to herself to "Open the book" is also a challenge to the reader, the traveler. The journeying of the traveler becomes a mapping of interior landscape, a project for which there is no easy resolution.

I fear that I have resorted to the easy dualities that we so often rely upon when discussing literary works – tourist poems versus travel poems; looking versus seeing; the worldly Europeans of Henry James novels versus the rough earnestness of his Americans; the Old World's valorization of culture versus the New World's more pernicious valorization of materialism. Yet the fact remains that nearly all poems of travel imply such dualities, and that the enduring works of the genre seek not just to explore these dualities but to obliterate them by breaking through their boundaries. And it is often at these boundaries between states – at these borders both metaphorical *and* national – where the best poetry becomes possible. To exist for a time at these junctions and margins is of course risky business, for it entails uncertainty. (Why do the guards look so closely at our passports? Why was the woman before us called into the back room?) At such border crossings we experience the moment when, as Jarrell's "The Orient Express" would have it, "a questioning precariousness / comes over everything." And it is this very precariousness that must precede the moment of gnosis when we have "looked our infant sight away." Yet to state the issues in this way is a bit grandiose, and the truest travelers are, like the poems of Elizabeth Bishop, self-effacing. The best written and most beautiful travel book I know of is Apsley Cherry-Garrand's unpromisingly titled *The Worst Journey in the World*. Cherry-Garrand, who used his inheritance to pay for a place in Scott's Antarctic expedition, had the dubious honor of discovering the frozen bodies of Scott and his companions. While remaining behind at the base camp while Scott and his party set out to conquer the pole, Cherry-Garrand and two associates planned a shorter expedition of less ostensibly heroic implications: a weeklong excursion to a nearby ice floe to obtain some emperor penguin eggs for scientific study. The trip in fact took nearly two months, and Cherry-Garrand and his party suffered unbelievable privations, returning to the base camp frostbitten, snow-blind, starved, and nearly toothless because of scurvy. This harrowing journey, recounted in the deadpan fashion so typical of British travel writing, occupies a good portion of Cherry-Garrand's six-hundred-page memoir. But it is only near the end of his account that Cherry-Garrand succumbs to the urge to philosophize, and at the close he offers a bit of advice to all prospective travelers: "You will have your reward, as long as all you want is a penguin egg."

STEPHEN COREY

"She is startled at the big sound": Poetry as Translation

[CHAUTAUQUA WRITERS' WORKSHOP]

For my daughter, Rebecca Elizabeth Yeong Ae

> *I suppose you could say nothing*
> *is easily said. Nothing.*

At this point in my life, I don't believe I could say anything about myself that didn't have something to do with why I am a writer and with what I have learned about *being* a writer. This is good news because it indicates the constant, all-encompassing nature of a commitment to an artistic vocation, but it is bad news for the same reason. Most artists are relentless in their pursuit of accomplishment and excellence in their given arts. This is not new news, yet it bears repeating because some awareness of this driving, not-always-attractive force is crucial – for the artists as they do their work and try to make some sense of it, for anyone else who cares about creation and creators.

One of the awful truths about artists – *awful* in both its modern sense of "terrible" and its more positive root sense of "filled with" or "inspiring" awe – is that although most sensitive people extract lessons in living from their experiences, artists are just as likely to take, from the same kinds of daily occurrences, lessons in art as well. Certainly a key question to be answered if we wish to understand the human impulse toward creating and valuing – and *not* valuing – art is this: What factors in the genetic and environmental makeup of individuals determine whether they will be overtaken, and taken over, by the urge to render their views of the world into analogous forms?

That said, I will admit immediately that my intentions here do not involve attempting to answer that question. Rather, I will assume the implied premise – that artists *are* a distinct group in underlying ways – so as to be able to examine certain things about how writers, myself and some others, behave and function in the world. At the heart of the conflicts between artists and nonartists throughout time – whether we speak of Plato's decision to ban poets from his Republic, Senator Jesse Helms's messianic need to remove them from the government's indirect payroll, or the countless marriages that have been cracked apart by this particular adamantine issue – is, I believe, the two groups' inability to comprehend or at least accept each other on the just-noted fundamental point of difference in their ways of seeing existence: The nonartist can seldom assimilate the visceral need of the artist to replicate the world, in stone or paint or print; the artist, having been driven slowly or rapidly into his career, cannot truly keep sight of the fact that nearly all the rest of humankind does not have *his* inclination – does not feel any desire whatsoever to head for studio or study at the occurrence of some important event, emotion, or thought.

On June 11, 1987, in Seoul, Korea, a female social worker named Hye Ryeong Lee filled out the "Initial Social History" form describing a six-week-old infant who would become, a few months later, my adopted daughter. Within a day or two, this document was translated into English by one J. J. Hong and then forwarded, via an American adoption-agency courier, to my wife Mary and me in Athens, Georgia – which is, quite literally, halfway around the world from Seoul. Thus, our first knowledge of this child who might be ours – we were free to accept or reject the "referral" – came not from a missed period or pregnancy testing or morning sickness, and not even from photographs; it came through words set down (however hurriedly or carefully we could not know) in one language and reworked (again, perhaps offhandedly or perhaps painstakingly) into another – the English that would allow us to make some sense of this vital information.

The first section of the form was titled "Identification," and its elements were small enough and straightforward enough that, for the most part, they gave us no pause over the matter of translation. "Child's Name": *Lee, Yeong Ae.* In our preliminary information-gathering about Korea, we had learned not only that last-name-first is the standard method of presentation, but also that an astonishing percentage of the populace has the last name Lee, so we were not surprised by anything here. Following Yeong Ae's name were her sex, case number (87C-1311), birth date (May 1, 1987, with 18:00 hours in parentheses as a bonus), birth place (the city of Taegu), date of admission to the adoption agency (May 9), race, and present location (foster home) – and none of these caused a hitch for us, either. The first little jolt came, I recall, with the final line of the identification section: "Meaning of Name." I was suddenly reminded that all of what we had just read so eagerly and quickly, and all of what was to follow in the two-page document, had begun in another language whose words and sounds we did not know and were not to experience here – except in the unaltered names of people and places. And all of *those* we were given only in Korean – except for the name of our prospective daughter, which we had now in both tongues: *Lee, Yeong Ae,* with *Yeong* (we were told) meaning "Light," and *Ae* "Joyful."

This designated and invisible infant, lying in a crib or on a lap eleven thousand miles away, was Light Joyful – or, as nearly any American would think immediately, Joyful Light. There was something invigorating *and* ominous about taking on a daughter with such a name, and I believe that both sensations emanated, in significant part, from my realizing that even though the name was strikingly attractive on the page – as translation – we never would have given it to any child we were naming, as it were, from scratch. The charm of the appellation resided somewhere on the immaterial path of its movement from the "there" of *Yeong Ae* to the "here" of *Joyful Light.*

As we continued to read through this initial pre-adoption report, the father in me was trying to gather every bit of relevant detail, stated and implied, that the relatively brief document had to offer. At the same time, the poet in me was increasingly moved and amused by the numerous ways the *translation* of information foregrounded itself in my mind – which is to say, by the ways that the particular wordings achieved by a non-native speaker of English asserted themselves *as language* to be savored and remembered for its exact configurations. We were told, for instance, that this infant girl had been placed in foster care at eleven days of age, and that "All the foster family members love Yeong Ae like a real child." So often, when we are taken up short by a translation, the point of agitation or pleasure is a single word slightly (or not so slightly) misused; in the sentence above, all is well except with that word *real*, which ought to have been *biological* or *their own*. Similarly, we were told of Yeong Ae's feeding that "after a bottle, she burps well without vomiting," and of her "toilet habit" (itself a dear phrase) we learned that "She moves the bowels once or twice a day in good condition. If she is wet, she cries, but refreshes herself with a new diaper stretching out the legs."

In these sentences, the curious roughnesses of translation become more numerous and complicated. With "she burps well without vomiting," the dissonance is again the matter of a specific word, since most native speakers of English would make a distinction for babies between "vomiting" and "spitting up" – although there is nothing technically wrong with the translator's choice of the former term. Likewise, there is an oddness in the final word of "She moves the bowels once or twice a day in good condition," even though contemplation and a trip to the dictionary reveal that one primary definition of *condition* is "a proper or healthy state." The nuances of our daily and colloquial uses of language are so interwoven and subtle that we can barely keep track of them ourselves, much less expect a foreign speaker to do so. "Refreshes herself with a new diaper" is one of the more amusing images projected here: the overly adult and sprightly verb that seems out of place in discussing a newborn, plus a reflexive grammar that gives the impression of a six-week-old infant changing her own soiled clothing and, perhaps, washing herself as well. There is also the small technical matter of an article being substituted for a possessive pronoun, so that Yeong Ae moves "the bowels" and stretches "the legs" – a difference which, for the native ear, inserts a curious distancing effect. Again, all of this reminds us of what a complex process every human being goes through in acquiring its primary tongue from infancy onward, and of the difficulties involved with becoming fluent in a language not one's own.

William Stafford, in his essay "Making a Poem / Starting a Car on Ice," has defined a poem as "anything said in such a way or put on the page in such a way as to invite from the hearer or reader a certain kind of attention." He then goes on to explain this particular instance of the wryly sage thinking for which he has come to be known: "This way of identifying a poem shies away from using content or form, or any neat means. It is not meter or rhyme, or any easily seen pattern, or any selected kind of content, or any contact with gods, or a goddess, that is crucial – it is some kind of signal to the receiver that what is going on will be a performance that merits an alertness about life right at the time of living it." Despite giving a first impression of vagueness and oversimplification, this definition of poetry has of late become one of my favorites; I love its whimsical wisdom, and even more I love its accuracy and truth value in the real world. Go spy wherever someone is holding a book of poetry in hand and reading silently, or – better still – go wherever two or more are gathered to hear poetry read or recited aloud. The body language and the focus of attention *are* different when an audience is offered poetry; even those who dislike it know, along with those who love it, that it occupies a special realm in our world of uses for words.

The specialness boils down, I believe, to phrasings (and occasionally ideas) that are distinctive and original, to intensified metaphorical thinking, and to rhythms that are pleasing and to some degree pronounced. Poetry is *not* generated by writing's content or themes, nor by the life circumstances of its author, nor by any personal, social, or political intentions of that author. All of these elements can be of great importance in supporting roles, but they have no parts to play unless the whole work is given life by the poet's love for, and exploration of, the properties and possibilities of language itself. Everyone with a tolerably decent education, one that included *some* exposure to poetry and the other arts, has subsequently had the occasion to note bits of special language – in a child's babbling, in a television news broadcast, on a roadside sign, in his or her own thoughts. Of these bits we often think or say, "That's *poetry*," or "That's just like poetry." So, I would be making no intellectual or linguistic waves – no poetry, if you will – were I to claim here that I found poetry in Yeong Ae's translated social history. I did find it, but that is not my news for the day.

My news concerns what came to me in the months after my first reading of that document, what has not shaken free from my thoughts even though now (in 1993) some six years have passed since its arrival. The tuning fork that has continued to vibrate, the hole that has continued to open beneath me – these were only hinted at by what I have quoted from that report thus far. Their strongest and finest moment came when I read the following consecutive statements about Yeong Ae's "Speech and Response Development": *"She is startled at the big sound. She is dazzled at the strong light."* That there could be something called "the big sound" in the life of a weeks-old infant, and that that same tiny child could be "dazzled" – for me, these are the kinds of truths that render the human mind magical, that allow me to believe (if only for a moment) in those fragile things we must have to survive in a harsh world: pleasure, hope, beauty, innocence, meaning.

J. J. Hong was not, I am sure, trying to be a poet when translating Hye Ryeong Lee's original evaluation into English. She was merely trying to be as accurate and forceful as possible, given the gap (which she may well not have thought about) between her knowledge of English and that of a typical native speaker. But the gap she had to span was very much like the one a serious poet confronts every time he or she sets out to write. Robert Frost said, "Poetry is what is lost in translation" – meaning, I think, that poetry makes use of every element and combination of elements a language has to offer, and that to move such complexity and subtlety into a different framework is virtually impossible. Subsequently, another writer (whose name I have lost) refuted Frost with, "Poetry is what is *not* lost in translation" – which seems to suggest that the real core of poetry has something to do with its elements having an almost spiritual quality, one that survives any "superficial" changes such as the trip from one language to another.

I say here, "Poetry *is* translation" – which is to propose that all poetry worth having and keeping achieves the status of a language that is substantially *other* than the speaker's native tongue. Rainer Maria Rilke's poems are not written in German; Pablo Neruda's poems are not written in Spanish; Walt Whitman's poems are not written in English. To reach what we usually refer to as a "style" in poetry is to have created a new language, one that the poet did not know before and that the reader must learn if he or she is to enter that poet's work. The difficulty for the reader of such a language – and the pleasure as well – is that, like all things sui generis, it has no dictionary and no handbook of grammar and usage until the reader creates them with the help of the poems at hand. In this sense, the reader is like an anthropologist doing field study of a newly discovered, isolated people and their unique system of speech.

Ursula K. Le Guin asserts, at the beginning of her futuristic novel *Always Coming Home*, that "the difficulty of translation from a language that doesn't yet exist is considerable, but there's no need to exaggerate it." I believe what she is saying here is relevant to my point at hand, despite the seemingly very different context of her claim. What we are both trying to deal with is the aesthetic imagination in action, fueled by the need to make something that has never existed in quite the form it is about to take, and I think this becomes at least a little clearer if we follow Le Guin's line of thought further.

> The ancient Chinese book called *Tao teh ching* has been translated into English dozens of times . . . but no translation can give us the book that Lao Tze (who may not have existed) wrote. All we have is the *Tao teh ching* that is here, now. And so with translations from a literature of the (or a) future. The fact that it hasn't yet been written, the mere absence of a text to translate, doesn't make all that much difference. What was and what may be lie, like children whose faces we cannot see, in the arms of silence. All we ever have is here, now.

Something of the writer in me – perhaps even the attitude that made me a writer? – has always believed that a new language is the goal, the point, during the continually present moment that characterizes the process of artistic creation. For instance, about fifteen years ago (fairly early in my writing life) I wrote a three-part love poem whose second section, "What We Did, What You Will Know," goes like this:

> We invented a language
> you will never speak,
> but you will hear its diction
> in all I can write.
> Any scholar of my work
> will know, for every word,
> one less thing than you.
> You will know a candle means
> a tall gray bookcase,
> any small wound is a rug,
> and orange shirts are ropes
> that can pull us to places
> different from those we have known.

This poem has a primary and, I think, fairly straightforward life as an intimate, private offering passed from lover to lover. The only potential confusions or difficulties concerning this personal level of the poem's life arise, in the closing lines, from the very point the poem is making – but these problems remain only if the reader fails to be persuaded that what is being called for is emotional rather than lexical accuracy. I don't think I am pushing this lyric too hard, however, if I look back and see myself establishing a theory of poetry in the opening lines: "We invented a language / you will never speak, / but you will hear its diction / in all I can write." Especially if I toy around with the pronouns in this brief passage, I hear the style-as-separate-language claim I mentioned moments ago: the "you" becomes the reader, in collusion with the poet in this business of finding another realm where the ordinary – in language, and therefore in everything else – does not apply.

I would seem a simpleton if I were to suggest that any poem composed originally in English could be a "translation" in exactly the same sense as Robert Fitzgerald's re-creations of *The Iliad* and *The Odyssey*, or Richard Howard's versions of Baudelaire, or any of a hundred other superb renderings from one primary language into another. But I do want to suggest that a phrase I just used – "any poem composed originally in English" – contains a generally unacknowledged self-contradiction, or at the least a gross oversimplification. I would claim that if we think carefully about the deepest nature of poetry, we must realize there is no such thing as a poem written "in English." We can point toward specific elements in a poem – the individual words, the punctuation and capitalization (or lack thereof), much of the phrasing and syntax and grammar – and understand that *some* English is indeed contained within this particular space of language. But these pieces can no more signal or express the full nature of the poem than bowls of flour, water, and leavening can offer up an explanation of the loaf of bread sitting beside them on the counter.

To help explore this remark a little further, I want to lay out a few bits of poetry, some well known and some not. First, the opening lines of Gerard Manley Hopkins's "The Windhover":

> I caught this morning morning's minion, king-
> dom of daylight's dauphin, dapple-dawn-drawn Falcon, in his
> riding

> Of the rolling level underneath him steady air, and striding
> High there, how he rung upon the rein of a wimpling wing
> In his ecstasy! then off, off forth on swing,
>   As a skate's heel sweeps smooth on a bow-bend: the hurl and
>   gliding
>   Rebuffed the big wind. My heart in hiding
> Stirred for a bird, – the achieve of, the mastery of the thing!

Next, the beginning of one of Shakespeare's most harsh and convoluted sonnets, number 129:

> Th' expense of spirit in a waste of shame
> Is lust in action; and till action, lust
> Is perjured, murderous, bloody, full of blame,
> Savage, extreme, rude, cruel, not to trust;

Now, a bit of e. e. cummings once –

> anyone lived in a pretty how town
> (with up so floating many bells down)
> spring summer autumn winter
> he sang his didn't he danced his did.

– and cummings again:

> what if a much of a which of a wind
> gives the truth to summer's lie;
> bloodies with dizzying leaves the sun
> and yanks immortal stars awry?
> Blow king to beggar and queen to seem
> (blow friend to fiend:blow space to time)
> – when skies are hanged and oceans drowned,
> the single secret will still be man.

And to finish off this selection, some Emily Dickinson – two complete poems, since she is so brief and so brilliant, even in these out-of-the-way examples:

[5 4 6]

To fill a Gap
Insert the thing that caused it –
Block it up
With Other – and 'twill yawn the more –
You cannot solder an Abyss
With Air.

[5 9 9]

There is a pain – so utter –
It swallows substance up –
Then covers the Abyss with Trance –
So Memory can step
Around – across – upon it –
As one within a Swoon –
Goes safely – where an open eye –
Would drop Him – Bone by Bone.

In what sense or senses might the writings of these four poets be taken
as representatives of the same language? Well, certainly all the poems fit
together under the most sweeping of definitions that my dictionary *(Web-*
ster's New World: Third College Edition) provides for the word, such as "human speech" and "a system of vocal sounds and combinations of such
sounds to which meaning is attributed, used for the expression or communication of thoughts and feelings." And I suppose I would even have
to admit that these poems could be linked by the following definition as
well: "all the vocal sounds, words, and ways of combining them common
to a particular nation, tribe, or other speech community [the French *lan-*
guage]." However, I find the practical value of this "truth" to be akin to
that involved if I were to assert that the "language" I learned in my high-
school Spanish classes is the same one spoken in Lima, Peru, where I had
occasion to spend several weeks during 1992: many similarities exist between the one and the other, but a whole new set of mind and ear is called
for if we are to make our ways meaningfully through the works of a poet or
the streets of a foreign city.

One might argue that the poets I've chosen to quote here offer ex-
tremes in individuality of voice, particularly Hopkins and cummings. I
would concede the truth of this, but I would not see it as any diminishing
of my point. I've deliberately selected obvious examples so as to make
my point quickly, but we could look at all manner of first-rate poets and
discuss the special languages they have conceived – languages every bit
as complete as, even if more subtly presented than, the ones I've just
sampled. William Stafford himself, for instance, has mastered a decep-
tively simple grid of short lines and short sentences whose many breaks,
turnings, and stops reverberate in sympathy with his relentlessly quick
shifts from description to narrative to meditation to newly minted prov-
erbs. One can see flashes of this style in excerpts from nearly every poem
he has published . . .

> All those miles leading north,
> hands out for any leaf,
> through the cold nights, we walked
> while only the river moved.
>
> Long valley, no one, the wind
> wild like a rough friend –
> we never complained; it was good,
> hearty, expected to end.
> It did. We understood.

(from "The Conditions")

> When God watches you walk, you are
> neither straight nor crooked. The journey
> stretches out, and all of its reasons
> beat like a heart.

(from "Any Journey")

. . . and sometimes in whole works, particularly short ones such as "At the
Edge of Town":

> Sometimes when clouds float
> their shadows make dark fields,
> wings that open. Just by looking

we become them. Is there a kingdom
where only the soundless have honor?
Some days, yes. We look up and follow.

Even William Wordsworth, who in 1800 claimed in the famous preface to the second edition of *Lyrical Ballads* that his poems deploy the "language really used by men," manages nonetheless to create, as his writing life unfolds, a "language of Wordsworth" that is in fact quite distinct from common parlance – a language characterized by (among other things) a sonorous and slow-paced blank verse, and a narrative structure built on alternating passages of straightforward anecdote and lofty reflection. (We should not be surprised that Wordsworth wasn't as plainspoken as he liked to say he was, since that same preface also speaks of his belief that we must "throw over [his poems] a certain colouring of imagination, whereby ordinary things should be presented to the mind in an unusual way," and that he must "purify" the language of men of its "real defects" before putting it into his poems.)

Returning to the string of poets I have quoted – Hopkins, Shakespeare, cummings, Dickinson – I wish here only to point out some of the key elements that characterize their particular translations. The Jesuit priest Hopkins tried to help us read his language by actually coming up with new terms for describing what *he* thought were its distinguishing features: most notably, *sprung rhythm*, which "consists in scanning by accents or stresses alone, without any account of the number of syllables, so that a [metrical] foot may be one strong syllable or it may be many light and one strong"; *inscape*, "that 'individually distinctive' form (made up of various sense-data) which constitutes the rich and revealing 'oneness' of any natural object"; and *instress*, "that energy of being by which all things are upheld, that natural (but ultimately supernatural) stress which determines an *inscape* and keeps it in being." These definitions are in fact helpful, especially the first one about rhythm, but Hopkins's language is even more crucially defined by the wonderfully outrageous phrasings and metaphors his ear and his faith led him to concoct: the "dapple-dawn-drawn Falcon" from "The Windhover," the "stallion stalwart, very-violet-sweet" from "Hurrahing in Harvest," or from "Spring and Fall" the exquisitely beautiful mysteriousness of "Nor mouth had, no nor mind, expressed / What heart heard of, ghost guessed."

Shakespeare – how to try or dare to speak in a few sentences of such breadth and depth of genius? – seemed to understand as well as any other writer in history that the life of language's art is provided by constant variations woven upon the frames of central forms – dramatic, poetic, and so on – which themselves must be varied, though more deliberately, over time. He shows us that the strongest tragedy contains much comedy; that the sonnet, a form whose heart is the iambic pentameter line, is at its best when iambic pentameter is least consistently in evidence; that the abstract and the concrete make the most powerful bedfellows in a poem – though also the most dangerous, if they are not tucked in just so; and that the poet's control of rhythm – its hammering and swaying and whispering – makes or breaks his control of the reader's ear, and heart, and soul.

In "Th' expense of spirit" quoted earlier, wrong-minded love takes on a grotesque visage that culminates with a comparison to "a swallowed bait," and the iambic meter that dominates several of the lines is crosscut by a very high incidence of commas and semicolons – the effect of which is a jagged fragmentation that both suits the thematic content and causes this particular sonnet to feel much longer than its 140-odd syllables. (Also worth special note concerning Shakespeare's insistence upon variation and contrast is sonnet 73, "That time of year thou mayst in me behold," which has only one line of true iambic pentameter – and each of whose lines scans differently from the other thirteen.)

e. e. cummings invented words with such aplomb, and played with punctuation and syntax so radically, that he persuaded us it was all so simple as to be merely quirky, and even infantile. And indeed much of it was, but some of it bears the unmistakable stamp of original genius, if only we make ourselves see and hear it clearly enough. No accident, I think, that we can recall nobody like him before his time, and no accident either that now there is almost nothing so easy to spot as a cummings imitator. Again and again he takes us with him, in language, "somewhere i have never travelled,gladly beyond / any experience," to a place where "nobody,not even the rain,has such small hands."

Or, perhaps, the rain and Emily Dickinson – who, if poems could be measured according to some density factor determined by an equation involving overall word count versus number of profound and memorable phrasings, would almost certainly have to be designated the greatest poet in the history of the English language. Quickly setting aside all those dashes – which have been variously described as bold invention, avoidance of more complex and subtle choices, and a mere fluke of Dickinson's particular schooling – I believe what we must come to as *her* language, all the more foreign in practice for its sounding so familiar in theory, is an almost frightening richness of metaphorical thinking. Then, Dickinson links this wealth of brilliant analogies with her ability to create abstractions that feel like concrete objects (recall the abyss that appears in both of the poems I quoted above), and her complementary ability to turn the slightest of objects into the weightiest of symbols ("I heard a Fly buzz – when I died – ") without generating the aura of artificiality that usually accompanies such a move in the work of lesser poets.

One way I like to read a dictionary is as if it were an instruction manual that could tell me exactly how something should be done – that is, exactly how a word should and should not be used, and how it has been used in the past. Sometimes my ignorance is complete when I go to the dictionary, other times it is partial, and usually it turns out to be more complete than I had thought beforehand, especially concerning etymologies. Thus, I was interested to discover that the second definition of *translate* given in my *Webster's* is "to put into the words of a different language," since this is of course the meaning most operative in the foreground of all my essaying here. The *first* definition, however, is this: "to move from one place or condition to another; transfer," with specifics cited from ecclesiastical writings ("to transfer [a bishop] from one see to another" or "to move [a saint's body or remains] from one place of interment to another") and from theology ("to convey directly to heaven without death"). And the sixth definition, noted as being archaic, certainly would be found to have at least some connection to number one: "to enrapture; entrance."

These are aspects of *translate* that I and most any other poet would love to have operative in our poems as we forge them from a blend of the language we know and the one we must invent. Frost said, in concluding a poem about the balancing of one's life between the world immediately at hand and the realm beyond the treetops, "One could do worse than be a swinger of birches." I say, one could not do much better than to create a patch of language capable of reaching into and around the world – say, from Seoul to Athens, Georgia – with such force and surprise that it changes a life, or even many lives. What greater reward could one expect for stepping off into the silence and seeking the right words to begin to fill it?

Yeong Ae stares indefinitely at surroundings, when awake. She sleeps on the flank alternately. . . . She follows a strong colored object visually as it is moved. On the tummy she gets troubled turning the head side ways. If held in the standing position she presses the feet against the surface. Her crying is loud. She has a strong grip.

EMILY UZENDOSKI

So the Wind Won't Blow It Away

[NEBRASKA WRITING AND STORYTELLING FESTIVAL]

I want to share my Nebraska identity with you. I come from Nance County in central Nebraska and, in the past, even in prosperous times, my county has been regarded by the Nebraska Department of Economic Development as one of the poorer counties in the state and by the Harvard School of Economics as one of the poorest counties in the nation.

As you may have read in the newspapers, we in rural Nebraska are caught in a time of cataclysmic change. In the last fifteen years, we have been witnessing the collapse of the culture that I knew and experienced as a child. There simply aren't that many people left to carry out the rituals of humanness that we have had in our culture. For example, in Nance County, as the countryside continues to depopulate, our numbers have regressed back to the level of the 1890s. There aren't enough young people, physically able-bodied people, to carry on the rituals that convey and transmit the values that have always held rural small-town and agrarian culture together. And so we witness crack-up, breakup. The gesture that might have been made is not made, the visit that might have been paid is not paid, the words that might have been spoken are not spoken, the neighbor down the road is not there anymore. It reminds me of the closing lines of William Butler Yeats's poem "The Second Coming": "And what rough beast, its hour come round at last, / Slouches towards Bethlehem to be born?" We are waiting for some new culture to be born.

In our community—an approximately twenty-mile stretch of farm, ranch, and wilderness land along the north side of the Loup River called Pleasant Valley—we identify people by geography, by the topography of the land. You either live in the valley of the Loup River, or you are a hill person up in the hills, or you are from across the river. I come from the valley.

By way of identity, this twenty-mile stretch of valley is believed to be settled by three different categories of people. In valley folklore, the western end of the valley was settled by Southerners who came up to Nebraska after the Civil War. They are thought of as a rather romantic, wild people: they talk in Southern voices and practice chivalry and ride horses and have wild adventures. In regard to those who inhabit the center of the valley, I have heard these people respectfully referred to as the descendants of the D.A.R., Daughters of the American Revolution. In valley mythology, they have lived in America for two hundred years; they are mostly Anglo-Saxons; and like Hamlin Garland's family, they moved westward with the frontier: "Big Rock Candy Mountain" – the grass was always greener in the undiscovered territory – but they stayed in the valley. At the eastern end of the valley, where my family is from, this, in the ancient folk history of the valley, is where mostly foreigners live. We are the Poles and the Germans who came late to America in the 1870s. We were the foreigners. My mother as a child, living in a neighboring county, was sent to school speaking Polish, her first language, for which she was ridiculed by other children. To this very day, I can remember how my mother – she would do this yet in the 1970s – would beat her fist upon the dinner table, would pound the dinner table, saying: "We are Americans! We are Americans! We are not foreigners. We are not foreigners!"

Just to bring you up to contemporary times in Pleasant Valley: In my childhood I witnessed or lived through the Dog Wars. These wars are part folklore, part legend, part tall tale, but actually, in folk fashion, truth, also. The people in the valley have always had a problem wearing the cloak of civilization. I think it is because we have so much wilderness. Farm and ranch enterprises exist side by side with the large amounts of wilderness because of Loup River with its Wildcat Islands and the myriad creeks that run down the canyons from the rising hills above, descending the flood plain to launch their waters into the river. So the people had trouble putting on the mantle of civilization. If you got angry at someone, the custom was you went and shot their dog. And the individual who had his or her dog shot would sit and think: "How many people want to get even with me? Who did I piss off?" The individual with the dead dog usually had a list of two or three possible neighbors who might have shot his or her dog. So, to uphold honor as the valley code requires, that individual would go forth and shoot two or three dogs. Then the owners of these dead dogs would think the same way – Who shot my dog? And this would ricochet down the whole valley until the last dog was dead. This was not so bad until lately, because in those days most farm dogs were mongrels and mutts and they could be readily replaced; but, after the coming of television, the power of this medium started to change the culture, and sometime in the mid-1970s the observance of status symbols started coming into the valley. People started spending as much as two hundred dollars on status-symbol dogs, so now it is a very expensive business to have a dog war.

So that is where I am from – Nance County. The valley along the Loup River – Pleasant Valley.

I chose to title this speech after a novel by Richard Brautigan: *So the Wind Won't Blow It All Away.* It is set in the 1940s after World War II, and its narrator tells a tragic story of how his childhood came to an end and of all that was lost. On the cover of the hardbound edition, there is a picture of a sofa, a rocking chair, a television set, a living room table on which a brightly shining lamp and family photographs are sitting on a lace doily – all parked in the wilderness along a pond. Part of the novel's cast of characters is a family – but only the mother and father because their children and lifelong friends have moved away. Daily, they haul their living room furniture by pickup truck to the shore of a pond and set it up to fish while sitting on their living room sofa. Of them, the narrator speaks:

> I sat there watching their living room shining out of the dark beside the pond. It looked like a fairy tale functioning happily in the post–World War II Gothic of America before television crippled the imagination of America and turned people indoors and away from living out their own fantasies with dignity. In those days people made their own imagination, like home-cooking. Now our dreams are just any street in America lined with franchise restaurants. I sometimes think our digestion is a soundtrack recorded in Hollywood by the television networks.

That's pretty profound, if you think about it.

The narrator's vanished childhood and the child's lost world speak to the transitory nature of mortals and of the values they expressed in their lives and of the disappearance of entire worlds or cultures in the American past. "Dust... American... Dust" is the novel's evocative refrain of an American past that exists now only in memory.

Another writer, Louise Erdrich, pointed out in her *New York Times Book Review* essay, "Where I Ought to Be: A Writer's Sense of Place," that "Americans don't inhabit a landscape long enough to understand it," that "Western Culture is based upon progressive movement," and that Americans feel "nothing, not even the land, can be counted upon to stay the same." Contemporary writing, Erdrich notes, is less likely to be set in an "unchanging landscape combined of myth and reality... enlivened by a sense of group and family history."

Instead, she observes, landscape in contemporary writing is moving toward "that which may be cheapest and ugliest in our culture, but which may also have an austere and resonant beauty in its economy of meaning. We are united by mass culture to the brand names of objects, to symbols like the golden arches, to stories of folk heroes like Ted Turner and Colonel Sanders, to entrepreneurs of comforts that cater to our mobility, like Conrad Hilton and Leona Helmsley. These symbols and heroes may annoy us, or comfort us, but when we encounter them in literature, at the very least, they give us context." She further notes that "brand names and objects in fiction connote economic status, upbringing, aspirations, even regional background." This cataloging has replaced the portrayal of physical landscapes deeply rooted in a sense of place. Dismayed at this trend, Erdrich points out that place is identity – our sense of place is our identity. She asserts that "through a study of a place, its crops, products, paranoias, dialects and failures, we come closer to our own reality." She urges us as writers not to "abandon our need for reference, identity or our pull to landscapes that mirror our most intense feelings."

I would now like to move to the major point of my talk today, which echoes a belief of Elie Wiesel, a witness to the Holocaust and recipient of the Nobel Peace Prize. Wiesel said, "Not to transmit an experience is to betray it"; "Nothing threatens and diminishes man more than silence." Think about it – *not to transmit an experience is to betray it*. We have a duty, Wiesel says, to transmit our experiences.

Each one of us has our own individual experience of reality. Our writing is our interpretation of it. And, Wiesel says, we must "shatter the silence." Break the silence. We have this duty to transmit our experiences.

And when I think today of Nebraska, I think of how our culture in rural

Nebraska – the little towns, the farms and the ranches, the land-people – has been disappearing in the last fifteen years. The disappearance and breakdown has been enormous. We must preserve our memories of the values and beliefs and customs that are vanishing before us – becoming, to quote Brautigan again: "Dust... American... Dust."

My parents have told me that it wasn't so bad during the Depression because family and relatives lived close to one another and sons and daughters didn't move away and because the people in the community were together as a community: the people got together a lot, shared possessions a lot, still had parties, still were a group, still worked together. Today the depopulation, the leaving of the younger generation, is breaking this cultural continuity.

Wiesel has said that "our fate is never ours alone." We share a collective fate. As humans, as part of the human community, we share a collective morality. Even though Wiesel is speaking out of the context of the Holocaust, I believe his observation pertains to us, especially to those of us who are writing autobiographical stories, family stories, memoirs, or reminiscences. We write and tell our stories as survivors. We are alive. As Wiesel points out, the death of a single person is the death of an entire world. Wiesel says that to write as a survivor is to write as a witness to what was, to speak as a witness for the dead. We tell the stories of our families, our family histories; we write autobiographies and memoirs; we write as survivors. We are the ones left alive to tell the story. Wiesel says that survivors do not create – they re-create. Their challenge is to re-create a world that is gone. They re-create the dead.

I believe this theme is very important: writing across generations. The older generations have this duty to pass on family stories, to re-create the world that has disappeared, that is gone. The histories of our families, our family stories, are the first literature that our children hear, according to sociologist Elizabeth Stone. Telling or writing these stories is the ritual that transmits the values of our culture – our beliefs, our humanness, our identity as members of a family, as members of a community.

This is one family story I tell. In 1965, there was a terrible drought that hit Nebraska. At that time my brother was in college, and he was driving from Nance County to Lincoln. It took him twice the usual amount of time because huge swirls of dust blew across Interstate 80. He told stories of drivers stopping to wipe the dust off their windshields. His trip necessitated a telephone call home to tell our parents of his safe arrival. I talked to my mother, and I asked, "Is the topsoil on our farm blowing away?" She paused for a moment, and she said, "No, it's all right . . . we can still see the stars." I didn't understand at first. I thought, What is my mother talking about? I ask her if our topsoil is blowing away, and she says, "It's all right! We . . . can . . . still . . . see . . . the stars!" I asked her what that meant, and she said, "During the thirties, the dust was so bad that it blocked the stars from view. We couldn't see them." And so when she said it was all right, she meant that the natural order had not been subverted. As long as you can see the stars, you still have the natural order and things are okay. It's not chaos; it's not disaster; it's not catastrophe yet. The stars were her psychological touchstone.

When we write our stories, we must reach down beyond the level of superficiality. Go for the psychological touchstones of our culture. Go for the archetypes if you can – the people who represent archetypes. Archetypes express our aspirations, our dreams, our hopes, our fears. When you write and tell your stories, go for the values and the beliefs and the customs of the culture. Go for the humanness of the people.

I would like to read a passage from a short story I have been working on – this is a work in progress – as a modest example of this kind of writing. It is set in Pleasant Valley in the mid-1970s. The narrator has returned to the family farm after being gone for a number of years and finds that it is the end of everything – the end of the farm, the end of a way of life, the end of a world. And presiding over the farm is the elderly father who dispenses justice. He rules the domain. The domain is the domain of the wild and the tame: the wild plants, the domesticated plants, the wild animals, the domesticated animals.

This is the old major theme of Western American literature of the frontier: the conflict between the wilderness and the garden in the grassland. Remember that when the Europeans came to America, their goal was to build gardens in the wilderness. Gardens. To farm is to garden. A garden walls things out: it walls out the wild things. A garden is very judgmental. It says: These plants are good, those plants are evil. The walls around a garden are to hold back the wilderness, which the first Puritans found very threatening. The Puritans, when they first came to our shores, as you remember, were horrified by the wilderness, terrified of it. It was filled with strange and howling beasts. They were scared of its fecundity: it was so thick, so dense.

The conflict has always been how to live in harmony with the wilderness. If you tame the wilderness, you destroy it. So this conflict is a reality – where wilderness and farming and ranching enterprises exist side by side.

Her father speeded up the car. Rose now engrossed herself in the geography of the land. To the north, the sumac-layered canyons were carved streaks of scarlet red between the rising hills. Straggly wind-driven timber lined in and out among the sumac: all taller things seeking the canyons for moisture and protection against the myriad winds. The hills were covered with grasses, combinations of native vegetation and foreign imports such as the Sudan grass of Africa. The grasses on the open hills were equal to the trickster winds. But much had not been in the valley; that is, much that had emigrated to the valley had not endured. So constantly sweeping in and out of Rose's vision were the ghostly houses of the failed ones, the bankrupted families who had left. Succeeding droughts and economic recessions had rained upon their heads; and so, in fleeing the valley the crushed ones had left the graveyard artifacts of abandoned homes and animal lodgings. For twenty miles along the valley road, for every living house, there stood five or more dead, unburied ones. Rose, like the other children of the surviving valley inhabitants, had grown up accustomed to looking at these corpses of defeated dreams, these unavoidable mirrors reflecting back the perversity of providence. And so, to the valley people in the best of times, these dead homesteads told forth the story of the worst of times. Lest, as the saying goes, lest they forget. Rose's father had always put it differently. Lest they get too brave – that is how he always said it. She had grown up learning there was a line between being brave and being too brave. Too brave was foolish and destruction. Not brave was cowardice and destruction. She had often pondered this mystery. After all, she reasoned, how was one to know the right brave, the correct degree of it?

They had ridden the valley road in silence, and now the car with its three passengers turned off the gravel into the family's private drive. It was a long thin road with three perfect acute turns in it, carrying them over a half mile into some off-centered center of their property. Rose loved this drive in the late-afternoon October sun. On each side the unharvested corn forest grew up to the very narrow road, creating a narrow tunnel through which the humans could pass. The dense yellow-brown corn plants towering in the whereabouts of eight to ten feet blocked out by their height and density all other noncorn life. Their musty smell permeated the air, and the natural dust off their bodies commingled with the stirred dust of the drive, causing a blurring effect on the eyesight, on all the senses; for the corn giants in their dense grandeur were always felt as well as seen.

Her father slowed up the car noticeably as they neared the encircling battery of trees that announced the outer perimeter of the homestead. There was nothing separating the corn from the trees, Rose noted: the corn forest simply grew up against the trees. Her father steered the car through the entrance in the trees and they were now coasting in the open air of the farmyard. Rose closed her eyes to block off the sight of the encircling buildings. Decaying and unkempt. She hated the pathetic ugliness of their deterioration. As they coasted to a stop in front of the aged white farmhouse, her father began yelling, "Rose, don't look! Run inside! Don't look! Hurry up! Run!"

His voice was loud and urgent. She fumbled for her suitcase, for the door handle, and tried to make herself rush through the old iron gate and gain the door of the porch. The anguish and anger carried from his voice finally roused the blind obedience of childhood, and she ran, hanging on to her suitcase, ran to the safety of the house. All the time wondering, What is it? What is it? Her mother followed, but not so fast. Her father was now shouting at the dogs. "Black Bear! Yellow Bull! Get out of here! Get out of here, you two dogs! Bull! Bear! Get out! You hear me! Get out!"

She turned and looked through the glass of the porch door. Her mother, seeing her looking, said simply, "He doesn't want you to see."

"What is it?" she asked.

"The sow and piglets died at birth, that's all. He didn't do anything with the bodies. Just left them lie in the shed. Now the dogs got to them," her mother said. "He didn't want you to see," she said again.

Rose understood. She was not to mention the dead piglets or the fact she had indeed seen Black Bear and Yellow Bull playing with their stiff pink baby bodies, carrying and tossing them about. She sensed there would be no more home-grown family pigs for her mother's marathon dinners. No more pigs, she thought, and grabbed her suitcase. But the image of Black Bear with the dead piglet in his mouth as the big shepherd came charging across the yardway remained with her, all the way up the staircase to the upstairs hallway.

At the top of the stairs, Rose paused long enough to listen to the telephone ringing. Then she stepped into the doorway of her brother's childhood bedroom. I have come home, she thought. After thirteen years in pursuit of worldly life, it has come to this, she thought. She only faintly remembered leaving the valley at the age of seventeen. All the while she was staring straight before her: her head tilted upward to meet the piercing brown eyes of the great deer. The great deer, preserved in the form of a mounted head, looked out into the hallway from her brother's childhood room. He looked out mostly at the rows of hunting guns lining the walls of the stairwell.

Rose walked toward the great deer and paused before his wild grace, retained in the carriage of his head and antlers and the glorious beauty of his face, his throat, the perfect alignment of his head upon his crested neck and the seeking look of his eyes. Reverently, she slowly reached her right hand upward until after a pause, she gently touched his muzzle and softly caressed his left cheek. Great deer, she thought, I have never, never forgotten the death of your body. She had not been there to witness, but had the story from her brother. And when her brother had married and gone to live in his own house on his own land, her father and he had quarreled over the mounted head of the great deer. But under no circumstances would her father let the great deer leave the old house.

Shatter the silence! Break the silence! Have courage to write the truth. Each time you write, swear as witnesses in court are asked to do: to write the truth, the whole truth, and nothing but the truth.

What I want to say to you is: Reach down deep. Reach deep for the psychological touchstones. What did it mean to live in a particular place at a particular time in history? What was it like to experience growing up as a child in a particular landscape or culture? Give your interpretation of reality. Only you saw what you saw, heard what you heard, felt what you felt. Only you.

And remember what Elie Wiesel said: "Not to transmit an experience is to betray it." Transmit your experience to younger generations . . . so the wind won't blow it away.

HERMAN DE CONINCK

Sex, Lies, and Poetry

[ASPEN WRITERS' CONFERENCE]

Translated by Stephen Smith

What makes a bad poem bad?

The question is as difficult to answer as "What makes a good poem good?" Why is "I have been one acquainted with the night" a beautiful line and "I've been boozing the whole night" not? I can give an answer to this, of course. It's my profession. But it would be about as exciting as answering the question: Why is it dark when the lights are out?

Naturally, this is simplistic. It's more difficult when you compare two relatively good lines, yet find that one is just a little bit better than the other. Why do I find "Thinking of death, I cannot sleep / and not sleeping I think of death" (just a little bit) less interesting than "My mother is an ashen Friday morning"? To me, this is completely subjective. I prefer images to ideas in a poem, and perhaps my own father was a merciless Monday morning. Something like that. Real objectivity doesn't exist.

Yet 90 percent of the time it does.

As a magazine editor, I receive perhaps a hundred poems a week. Ten of them I put aside, because I hesitate. To be completely certain of their value, I want to show them briefly to another editor. With one of the ten, I am fairly confident: This is a beautiful poem. Concerning the other 90 percent, I haven't any doubts: These are bad. I don't have to show them to anybody: they are *objectively* bad. (I'm certain of this because I *do* let other people read them.)

In 9 percent of the cases, then, subjectivity plays a role. Bias and personal taste are involved. Such is also the case for that one undeniably good poem. I am not, for example, any too moved by the poetry of T. S. Eliot, but most of his poems are strong enough to rise above that lack of empathy.

More interesting, and also more easily answered, than the question "What makes a bad poem bad?" is the question of how it comes about that you usually, inescapably know it's bad after the first two lines. Or even after having read the accompanying letter.

When Theo Sontrop, director of Arbeiderspers, a Dutch publishing house, once returned a novel he had been sent the very next day, the author reacted indignantly: Sontrop could not possibly have read the manuscript with the proper attention in so short a time. Sontrop nobly admitted to this, saying that he had only read one page, "But if after three licks of an ice cream I am left with a nasty taste, I don't eat the rest of the ice cream, either."

For the sake of convenience, let's assume there are three sorts of very bad poetry.

The first is a kind of vomiting poetry. The motto here is the more the merrier; ten adjectives are better than one. (What did I buy that great big dictionary for otherwise?) And those ten adjectives usually come from the list of unwieldy words. The poet can scarcely move them around and therefore lets them thud into the middle of a sentence. "The mountain stream spewed to the bottom. The sperm of the Milky Way. The train spurted through the night like a long ejaculation." No. These examples are still far too amusing. Everything should be firmly lodged in the power of five. Wait! A quick look at some recent copy. Here. An example already. About an executioner who murders a poem. Unfortunately, the poet does not realize that he is writing about himself.

> With his clumsy hands
> the executioner strangled the poem
> crushing its letters with powerful jerks
> of his merciless, murdering, monstrous,
> barbarian hands.

This kind of poet assumes that a text becomes stronger if you type on the keys with a sledgehammer. The only result, in fact, is that your typewriter gets broken. I call it "vomiting poetry" because it actually vomits three times: it's usually about disgust and aversion; it simply vomits those feelings out; and it also vomits out words. Unity of form and content – a double zero. The voltage is excessive. The fuses of the language blow, and the lights go out.

The second sort is love poetry – by preference unrequited. I know plenty of people who never read any poetry, but then become seriously ill, have a breakdown, lose a loved one – to death or to a rival – and then suddenly begin, not only to read poetry, but also to write it. Likewise, acquaintances rarely consult me about poetry unless they want to know which poem they should put in a funeral notice. I have always explained this to myself by assuming that in these cases the regard is mutual: in a society of helter-skelter progress, of looking forward, of "making it," and of profit, poetry is the only thing that occupies itself with looking back, nostalgia, bereavement, and death.

Whatever the case, whenever people who have previously never written are inspired by such events to suddenly start, it invariably results in bad poetry. They think they can suddenly write laments in a language previously reserved for professional memos. They see the symbol of their uncompleted lives in a cup without a handle. And then you can count yourself lucky, because they already know what imagery is. Take a happy poem:

> Never
> can I tell you
> how much I love you.
> Feel it in my body,
> drink it from my mouth.

Well, well, I think to myself. So you can't tell it. That much is obvious. But making it *so* obvious is no longer poetry. And what about the last two lines? "Feel it in my body, / drink it from my mouth"? As it happens, I know the address of the poet in question. But I don't think I ought to take her up on it. It wasn't directed at me, after all. So why did she let me read it?

The third sort is cosmic poetry. It tries to say too much, and ends up saying nothing:

United
with you, with you, with you
nature, the soil, the sea
Elementary forces
Life – life
Universe, cosmos, space
Brief
separation, rupture, pain
Pain – pain
Growing
Progressing
starting again
United, united, united
with you, with you, with you
organically
cosmically.

This isn't a poem, but a list, an outline from which to one day really write something – if you run a literary club and have a couple of centuries to spare. Because naturally, it's not an easy task. I couldn't think of a subject that's *not* included here.

These three sorts of very bad poetry have quite a lot of misconceptions in common. The misconception, for instance, that great emotions automatically give rise to great poetry. On paper, unfortunately, we only find Os and exclamation points. The great wind of Nothingness blows through them.

Poetry is simply not the same as emotions, ideas, and reality. If that were the case, you wouldn't actually have to write such poetry down. It would already be there, everywhere. Poetry *does* something with these elements. It uses them for its own ends. In fact, you can create certain emotions and ideas in a poem without having experienced them yourself: you don't have to be in love to write about desire, or know anything about physics to write about the Milky Way. In any case, lesser emotions are often a better guarantee of good poetry than terribly large ones. The more tears, the less vision. The misconception is that poetry somehow arises from those tears, when in fact it is something that helps us *against* those tears: a sort of windshield wiper. Further, I want to hear something in a poem, a falling pin, for instance. But what I hear is the fart of a brontosaurus. Lights out and, what's more, eardrums shattered.

A correct mixture of distance and involvement is needed in poetry. There's too much involvement, for example, in adolescent poetry. You are too close to your feelings. The words have no freedom of movement. On the other hand, too much distance can be found in some language poetry: whole fields of linguistic tension. But what was the subject again? I've forgotten. In both cases, little is revealed to the reader. In the first case, nothing at all. In the second, only some language. Too much involvement, then, is clearly the greatest danger to poetry. That's why, for example, the most "committed" poetry is so bad.

And that's why love poetry – successful love poetry – is of the highest order, because it's the most difficult to write (said the love poet). For a start, it has to be original. Half the poetry in the world is about love. And that, with a slight exaggeration, means you have to read it all in order to know what you certainly should no longer attempt to write. But what should you write? "Your hair is as blond as... your eyes are as blue as..."? The difficulty with a comparison is that in order to make it, you have to be able to *see*, and love is blind. And you must see not only the loved one, but also that to which you are comparing him or her. "Your eyes are as blue as the sea of..." You have to travel the world as well.

And you have to eliminate, ruthlessly: "Your eyes are like shimmering fish, no; like deep pools, no; like fjords, no; like marbles, no." Will it ever be bloody good enough?

In short, love poetry requires such a sober approach that you had better only write it when you are not in love.

Moreover, bad love poetry is not written for the general reader, but for one particular reader only. Up to that point, everything is in order. Problems arise, however, when these poems are sent out to magazines, nevertheless.

After poetry readings, I am often asked: "Sir, do you write for yourself alone, or do you write for the public?" The latter sounding a little disdainful, as if one must therefore make improper concessions.

But poetry that is written without the public in mind is not poetry. It's an emotional shopping list for my wife, a joke that nobody else can appreciate, because nobody else knows our secret language or can understand a personal allusion.

I'm certain of this because I've written rather a lot of love poetry my-self, with snatches of autobiography, dialogue, and jokes. And here I'd like to shock the sensitive reader a moment by admitting that these were all hackwork, effect-seeking, and calculation. I never actually spoke any of the written dialogue, never cracked any of the jokes. And it's rather ob-vious why.

To begin with, one never writes love poetry during the act, but before or after. It is either over, or yet to come, or it never happens. That's also possible. In these three cases, you have to call the experience up again, through your writing. And calling up is not the same as calling out. (Mis-conception three.)

Besides, too much love poetry can damage a relationship, because all of that passionate scribbling takes place at night, after your spouse has gone to bed alone.

If I should say to my wife (on paper): "Shall we do what we can?" not a single reader would know what I meant. That sentence dates from the days when we were trying to conceive our daughter. Someone we were visiting one evening remarked on the subject: "Man does what he can, God does what he will." To which my wife, instead of asking "Shall we be on our way?" asked: "Shall we do what we can?"

(Even this is a lie: the example comes from a lady neighbor.)

If I want to make jokes in a poem, then, I have to invent other jokes the reader will understand. And better jokes, too, and stronger dialogue. In private, I can make do with inanities. After all, I don't have to conquer my wife anymore. Well, perhaps just a little every night. But I do have to conquer the reader, completely, all in one go, and what's more, usually in less than fourteen lines.

On top of that, not just any old event will do. I have to describe one, preferably, that also has a little symbolic surplus. And if I am already busy inventing things, I might just as well, for the same effort, invent my auto-biography.

In short, it all boils down to lying as honestly as possible. And that's the way it has to be. If I were only to write, "Oh, oh, I'm so in love," the reader would think: Perhaps you are, but not me.

> I taste the kindness
> on your lips

> power shimmers through
> your body
> tenderness flows from
> your hands
> every little hair expresses
> pleasure
> you are love.

An infallible criterion for bad poetry is that the reader, after every statement, has a tendency to ask, "Yes, but so what?"

Misconception four is that a poem has to be about a subject. It can be. But then, something first has to happen to that subject, that fact, that thought, those feelings.

To again shock the sensitive souls who have not yet given up: The content of a poem does not interest me.

I once had a discussion with a formalistic poet who distinguished between two sorts of poetry. The first is autobiographical, in which you know before you start roughly what to say and then simply write it down. With the second sort, you know nothing in advance and only discover it as you are actually writing. Only the latter sort of poetry interested him.

Well, me too. I just don't see the difference. The fact is, I don't agree that poetry that is autobiographically inclined (like mine) is primarily concerned with content, with accuracy and truth, and that there is less happening with the language than in so-called language poetry—as if the latter term were not redundant.

Perhaps I am actually too lazy to look for subjects elsewhere, beyond my own experience, my own life. As a journalist, I roamed around for thirteen years looking for things to write about. For my poetry, I'd sooner stay at home. But not because I want to jot down quickly what I'm thinking. Always starting with the question, "What exactly *am* I thinking?" I write in order to find out. And I hope, in so doing, I will never find out.

If I want "real" content, I read the newspaper, or an essay, or nonfiction. As far as poetry is concerned, after the ultimate sentence, "People die and are not happy," there's nothing more you can possibly say. Unless it's the unsayable, and how you can never say it—though sometimes, *almost*. For instance, if you pretend that such is your aim at all.

What interests me in a poem is what gets added along the way. A good poem is also usually about something other than its ostensible subject. Often about poetry itself. The superficial content is no more than a sort of fishing net with which you try to catch a more essential, but more elusive, subject matter.

In nature poetry, this is rather obvious. You describe a leafless tree in winter, but you're actually writing about loneliness, growing old, dying off. You write about the moon, but your real subject is feminine charm. About a cactus, when you're really talking about a prickly, wizened old man. You don't want to say this too obviously, otherwise the reader can no longer *find* such meanings for himself. But you never write to impart something you already know. That's not interesting. You write in order to find out something. I write in order to discover what the advantages of being middle-aged could be. None, I presume. But I do my best. I try to manufacture acceptance – acceptance of being middle-aged – because I do not accept it. If I did, there would be no problem. But then there would probably be no poetry, either. I try to create an attitude for myself.

This attitude is more important than the actual content of my poems.

I read poetry because I am searching for attitudes. Death will come soon. How do you face it? I have no attitude. But through my own and primarily through other people's poetry, I try on a couple, like suits from the wardrobe. It's not a lot, I know, but an attitude is all you can really have toward great, dramatic events. And thanks to poetry, at least I can try on a few. Do I want the rather defiant tone of John Donne? ("Death, be not proud, though some have called thee / Mighty and dreadful, for thou art not so.") Or do I prefer the matter-of-factness of Sylvia Plath? ("Dying / Is an art, like everything else. / I do it exceptionally well.") Or the rage of Dylan Thomas? ("Do not go gentle into that good night.") I can choose.

The most fundamental attitude that lies at the foundation of all good poetry – at least, I think so – is the almost dandyesque attitude: Do or say whatever you like, drop dead at my feet if you must, but do it at least with style. Life itself has no style. Style is what you have to add. There is a consolation inherent here, which might not actually amount to very much, but which I wouldn't miss for any amount of money: We *are* going to die, but we'll do it at least with a beautiful text.

Finally, poetry is of course about something. Even about everything at once. About the unsayable, about the moon and the stars, anything you like. Bad poetry may sometimes *appear* to be about the unsayable, because it fails to actually say anything. But in fact it is only about Marieke from the bakery, with whom the poet is hopelessly in love. Music lesson, fifth grade. Teacher plays a recording of Beethoven's Pastorale. Question: "What does that remind you of?" First answer: "Of a storm in the forest." "Excellent. And you, Johnny boy?" "Of Marieke from the bakery, sir." "What do you mean?" "Everything reminds me of Marieke from the bakery, sir."

Good poetry does the opposite. The ostensible subject is only the means to a greater, more wide-ranging meaning or content. It may even be Marieke from the bakery, as long as the poem can thereby say something about all of the women in the world. The concrete and particular are means to the abstract, never the other way around.

The image, especially, is a means to this. And I do not simply mean an occasional comparison for the sake of clarity, although that is always a welcome bonus, but the archetypal image.

Poets almost always carry around a couple of those images, searching their whole life for the right words to express what they mean. Because they almost always mean more than what we can possibly say about them. How many snow poems can be found in the literature of the world? How many moon poems? I, too, carry a number of images around. Mist. Existence. To have and to hold. What is that? What in God's name can you ever have in this world, except for words? What is snow? God's mercy? But I don't believe in that, and yet I have nevertheless written some half a dozen snow poems. What is water? Freud's amniotic fluid? No, I don't believe in Freud either, and yet I have written a couple of water poems, too. Finally, also, a woman. What is that? Poetry, what is that? I hope I never find out, and, likewise, I also hope to dissuade those who think that they do know.

What is an archetype? When I was in the army, in Germany, in far-off Siegen, the birthplace of Rubens, in the middle of nowhere, songs in which the word "home" appeared were constantly played on the cafeteria jukebox. It was the age of "The Green, Green Grass of Home" by Tom Jones, of "Let Me Go Home" by The Pied Piper. Obviously, the word "home" was more appealing than the tiny villages to which it referred. Why?

The great thing about this sort of question is that no answer is ever really the right one. The best answers only add to the mystery. And perhaps, in so doing, give answers to the other, as yet unvoiced questions. Just as every good poem gives an answer to the question: What makes a bad poem bad?

BRUCE DUFFY

The World As I Left It:
Or Revisiting The World As I
Found It

[AMERICAN LITERATURE TODAY SERIES AT THE
STICHTING JOHN ADAMS INSTITUT, AMSTERDAM]

Wittgenstein found facts, and pictures of facts, immensely mysterious. I must say I do too. Like him I'm puzzled by how facts and words refer to actual things in the world. And I'm equally puzzled by facts, or statements of fact, that do not refer to reality – by this I mean fictions.

Consider the phrase "the present King of France." France, of course, has no present king. The words make sense, but they conjure a nonexistent person, a linguistic unicorn. But – how strange when you think about it! – we can talk about this royal personage, can even play with his nonexistence. For instance, we can say, "The King of France is wise." Or, "The King of France is wild about the American actor Mickey Rourke."

I can see why apparently meaningful nonsense like this so intrigued Wittgenstein and Bertrand Russell. But what truly haunts me are the names of people who once actually lived – names for whom there once were living faces. Among other things, my book *The World As I Found It* (1987) reflects my puzzlement – my hauntedness, I guess – with names and facts and faces.

Take Ludwig Wittgenstein.

Who is this person – this name, I should say – in relation to the historical personage Ludwig Wittgenstein? And who is this historical person relative to the legends and memories (good or bad or faulty) of the various people who actually knew him? How do we even remember a man like Wittgenstein, who went through so many radical changes in his life? For that matter, how do we speak of "Wittgenstein's philosophy" when that philosophy also changed so dramatically—at times almost constantly? How, in short, do we think of a human spirit over time? Oh, and one final question: How does our memory of a person consort, or coexist, with the reality of what it was like to actually *be* that person—assuming, of course, that anyone but God or the person himself could ever know such a thing?

These questions were on my mind when I began *The World As I Found It*. Seven years later, when I finished the book, they continued to trouble me, and they still do. I guess they've been with me from the time my mother died when I was a child. *How does anybody just disappear?* And if they do disappear, never to return, where, for instance, does love go? I was eleven years old when my mother died, but that's when I began to see how memories get distorted and carved up. We don't just fight over who gets the family silver and mama's sacred ring: these are just physical manifestations—stigmata—of a deeper form of human dislocation and suffering. It's memory we contest so bitterly. With my mother's disappearance, I began to see who memories serve. I began to see how memories tell truths, and likewise how they elude, refute, disguise, and even lie. But, above all, I began to see how memories constantly change, coming as they do, like starlight, from vast distances—and coming then with inevitable distortions under the inconstant light of the present. But here: a paragraph from the very last page of my novel that bears on these problems:

At the end of a life people assign it a weight or a general trend, a moral trajectory. They ask whether it was sad or happy, failed or successful, asking this just as if there can be some consensus after the self as remembered is safely consigned to the common estate of history, which is ultimately everyone's destiny and thus everyone's business. Like a willing weather, the spirit moves through time, and against its time. Thus the spirit is dry when all outside it is wet, cold when all is hot and confused while all others are certain. The spirit wonders at this difference, while those outside see the spirit coming in the guise of a man and try to form an opinion of what the weather must be like inside, some saying calm, others saying stormy, and still others saying that it is an impertinence to ask and better not to know, though in fact nobody really does.

But WHY? That's the question people always ask me. Why did you ever do such a weird thing? Why a novel about Ludwig Wittgenstein?

Well, it was an eccentric undertaking. In fact, it reminds me of an outrageous short story by the Argentine writer Jorge Luis Borges that you may recall. I refer to Borges's story "Pierre Menard, Author of the Quixote." In it, we find one Pierre Menard, a French writer who strives not to create another Quixote but Cervantes's masterpiece itself: as if through some crazy inductive logic, Menard sets out on a quest to re-create every word of *Don Quixote*.

But how is Menard to reimagine – and finally write – *Don Quixote* in 1934? As the narrator of the story dryly observes, "The first method Menard conceived was relatively simple. Know Spanish well, recover the Catholic faith, fight against the Moor or the Turk, forget the history of Europe between the years 1602 and 1918, *be* Miguel de Cervantes."

In this sense, Menard's project somewhat reminds me of my own odd task in beginning to write *The World As I Found It*. How was I to *be* Ludwig Wittgenstein? And if I was to do that, what Wittgenstein – or, should I say – *which* Wittgenstein, would I be? Talk about jousting at windmills!

Pierre Menard at least had the advantage of being European. Whereas Menard had nearly three hundred years of history to forget, I had some one hundred years to learn. I likewise had to steep myself in modern philosophy and logic, in fine points of European custom and even in principles of trench warfare. Also, to immerse myself in works that deeply influenced Wittgenstein – books such as Tolstoy's *Hadji Murat* and Otto Weininger's *Sex and Character*.

But even wider cultural and historical gulfs separated me from Wittgenstein. Born into a family of great wealth and culture, Wittgenstein was a Catholic of Jewish extraction who spoke high German and fluent English; he came from an enormous family, was musically trained and studied philosophy at Cambridge. By contrast, I majored in English – I only minored in philosophy. I'm an only child from an Irish Catholic, thoroughly middle-class family. I can't read or speak German, am not even remotely musically trained, and at the time I wrote my novel had never set foot in England or even on the Continent.

Ignorance . . . overall unsuitability for the task . . . I was ready to begin!

Twelve years ago, when I stumbled upon the idea for *The World As I Found It*, there was no biography of Wittgenstein. In those days, the facts were scattered. Even fragmented, you might say, with big holes that looked to me like freedom.

Today, this has changed. Now we have two major biographies: the 1988 book by Brian McGuinness, and the Ray-Monk biography that appeared in 1990.

Nearly forty years this took – forty years of declassification before we had a biography of the man who is arguably this century's greatest philosopher! You could blame Wittgenstein's estate, I suppose, but the real reason is Wittgenstein himself, and no wonder. Here was a man who stood like the Day of Judgment over those who knew him. Worse, here was a man who rejected virtually every interpretation of his work, even by those intimate with his thinking. In fact, to know anything about Wittgenstein is to acknowledge that he would have rejected most, if not all, of what has been written about him and his work. In this long roll of the condemned I certainly include *The World As I Found It*.

Then there's the continuing controversy over Wittgenstein's sexuality. When I first began my research, this deeply constrained, this muzzled quality was what most struck me in the various memoirs I read. Their efforts to put across a plain, unvarnished account of what Wittgenstein said and did had precisely the opposite effect: if anything, these books are gospel stories, hushed, reverential, proprietary. If anything, his disciples reminded me of the early Christians. Here were people running through the catacombs with the sacred relics, one step ahead of the Romans. Indeed! Render unto Caesar what is Caesar's, and to God, well...

In their almost ritual apologies and self-abasements, in their deep discomfort with even *presuming* to speak about Wittgenstein, these books showed more compellingly than they ever could have described the pall Wittgenstein cast over those who knew him. Fortunately, I was not saddled with this burden. I felt like a boy with new boots atop a hill of unblemished snow! Here before me was a whole life that so far no one had dealt with in a comprehensive way.

Was it moral, what I did? Was it moral of Max Brod not to burn Kafka's manuscripts and papers as Kafka had instructed? I can't answer this question except to say that there are different forms of homage. As I saw it thirty years after his death, Wittgenstein was nobody's moral property. Like a man buried at sea, he was rightfully consigned to history.

But let me be plain here: I was disgusted – no, outraged is the word –

that, to some, Wittgenstein's life *was* clearly considered off-limits, was considered a form of intellectual, professional, and even national property. Except of course to the duly initiated, and even then with palpable constraints.

A revealing question for me now is whether I would have written the novel – if there would have been the same *reason* to write it – had there been a biography. No, I suspect not. But does this mean, then, that it was my aim to write essentially a fictionalized biography?

Not at all. As I saw it, being "first," if you will, put me in prime fictional territory. By leaving most readers no other single authority to turn to for the truth, the book would raise a lot of difficulty. Difficulty in reading it. Difficulty in deciding what it was and difficulty in deciding what was true and what wasn't.

While taking me to task for the "accountability of my sources," a recent critic blunders onto this tension in the book. He writes: "It is difficult not to be distracted by the wealth of historical detail [Duffy] has incorporated to guarantee that his Wittgenstein will be confused with the real Wittgenstein."

Ah! That liberating word, *confusion*.

To further confuse things, I rejected the advice I was given several times, namely, not to use real names – in short, to observe the gentlemanly tradition of the roman à clef. A writer whom I greatly respect found my failure to do this a grievous aesthetic error. So be it. For Shakespeare to write his plays about Julius Caesar or Prince Hamlet was not a bothersome thing in his day. Today, it is. In an era of experts and unprecedented specialization – in a time when I should say we cripple ourselves by ceding far too much to the wisdom of experts – a book like mine is bothersome, for some people bothersome to the point of being disorienting. For all our self-conscious, postmodernist poses, for all our irony and formal sophistication, for all our exposure to the strategies of modern and postmodern art, many of us still like our categories straight. We are bothered by confusions of fact and fiction. We are bothered by a novel that, say, in its prologue, adopts the seemingly trustworthy voice of a biography only to monkey with the facts: This is unsportsmanlike, like impersonating a rightful officer of the law. Be more radical and experimental! Be more conventional! When they rap my knuckles, critics seem to hold out these two alternatives, often seemingly at the same time. But, again, their advice enshrines what too many naively expect nowadays. Straight categories. Fiction as some literary substitute for the old Classic Comics. Above all, the epic, churn-'em-out complacency of that form I almost uniformly detest—"historical fiction." These by now are old tactics that do not trouble anyone.

While we're at it, why didn't I use footnotes? Believe it or not, in an early crisis with the book, my publisher's editorial board wanted me to fill the back of the book with them. Footnotes! I hit the roof! Does a general give away his battle plans? Does the heretic recant? To me footnotes *would* have been a profound aesthetic error, not to mention an act of cowardice. Happily, though, I convinced my wonderful editor, and as a compromise I added the preface.

But then came another small crisis. Apparently, a fact-checking copy editor called my editor almost in tears, exasperated to find pages covered with truths and errors . . . and, yes, even the troublesome King of France. What a mess. Much like life, *mais oui?*

Look, I hope this doesn't all sound too pat. For an author to say he always knew exactly what he was doing—now, that's a real fiction!

Of course I got it wrong. Still, some people feel that I got an uncanny amount right, an impression that frankly surprises me when I realize in many cases how little I knew and how much I made up. David Pinsent's diaries. Wittgenstein's father's letters, and most of Wittgenstein's letters, too. Wittgenstein's family—his sisters, brothers, his father. Wittgenstein's friend Max and the entire World War I sequence. All this and more I made up. In fact, writing the book has taught me this: No one knows, not even those who knew Wittgenstein. Maybe especially those who knew Wittgenstein.

At the risk of being indiscreet, let me share portions of two letters I've received. One comes from a niece of Wittgenstein—a very nice woman, incidentally. Nevertheless, she wrote to chastise me, saying, "Who ever really knew him? Who could presume to describe this man's inner self, even in a fiction-coated novel?"

Another letter comes from a woman who was actually there when Wittgenstein dictated his Blue and Brown Books. She writes, "I wonder at how little I came to know of Wittgenstein personally, considering how many hours I spent with him. We were close, but distant."

The ultimate unknowability and undecidability of anyone. If you've ever used maps and compasses, you know there is an error one must correct for in order to find true north. It is much the same with a novel, which quickly establishes an unspoken contract with the reader. One important part of this unspoken contract is how far the book deviates from reality; it may deviate a lot, even magically so, but the idea, always, is to find true north, or at least a possible true north, or multiple norths.

In this respect, my Wittgenstein – my character, I should say – represents many norths, or so I hope. I say this because he is, in ways, a composite. In his youth, for instance, I found myself imagining the brilliant and precocious poet, Rimbaud. I thought of the Rimbaud who wrote at the age of sixteen, "It is wrong to say: I think. One ought to say: People think me. I is someone else."

How like Wittgenstein, who writes in 1916, "The I, the I is what is deeply mysterious! The I is not an object. I objectively confront every object. But not the I."

On the Russian-front sequence of the novel I thought of Ezra Pound's friend and hero, the great sculptor Gaudier Brzeska. Brzeska dead at twenty-three, in 1915. With the force of a wave, with almost Homeric abandon, the French sculptor died in yet another fruitless assault against German machine guns. Like Wittgenstein, here was a young man who badly wanted to prove himself. Again, I found the story of one who sought to test ideas and flesh and beliefs against brute steel. Several months before his death, Gaudier wrote – chiseled – in the brutal capital letters he used in his sculptured manifestos: "HUMAN MASSES teem and move, are destroyed and crop up again . . . WITH ALL THE DESTRUCTION that works around us, NOTHING IS CHANGED, EVEN SUPERFICIALLY. LIFE IS THE SAME STRENGTH, THE MOVING AGENT THAT PERMITS THE SMALL INDIVIDUAL TO ASSERT HIMSELF."

Now hear Wittgenstein. On the Russian front a year later, powerless before this same impersonal will, Wittgenstein writes: "A stone, the body of a beast, the body of a man, my body, all stand on the same level. That is why what happens, whether it comes from a stone or my body, is neither good nor bad . . . I am my world."

Then there's the Tolstoyan Wittgenstein that we find during and after World War I. In his "What Is Art" phase, Tolstoy longed to give up vice and meat, to write stories anyone could understand and make shoes for the humblest peasants. Under this same spell, Wittgenstein, after the war, publishes his *Tractatus;* he renounces philosophy, gives up his vast fortune, then goes off to teach peasant children in a poor Austrian village. Was Wittgenstein repeating the life of Tolstoy? Is history, as Nietzsche said, endless recurrence?

I don't scorn the truth – or the biographer's art. I respect the biographer's great tact and judgment, probity and intuition. But, you see, my instincts are radically different; they tell me to mix up, forget, bury and burn – to recombine and fuse disparate elements in what perhaps was a more confused and deliberately irresponsible attempt to create a kind of universal life. By "universal life," I mean a life that finally goes beyond its seeming subject, or subjects. For me, you see, this is not finally a book "about" Wittgenstein or philosophers, but rather a creation story examining the very forms of life in this world I had found. That is, the world that *all* of us have found – the world we found and doubtless will find only in other disguised forms, as we end this dark century and enter the next.

At the end of his short story, Borges tells us that Menard managed to add several chapters to the saga of Don Quixote. Maybe I lost a few. Finally, I feel I lost my Wittgenstein. True, I knew only a character, but for me that character died, as characters do; as a friend and hero and guide, that character died four years ago, disappearing for me as mysteriously as the real Wittgenstein who died in 1951. Hence the title of my novel. As you know, *The World As I Found It* is Wittgenstein's title. For me, it could almost serve as the great philosopher's epitaph. Or anybody's epitaph, I suppose.

Since they are so haunting and beautiful, here are Wittgenstein's own words from the *Tractatus:*

> If I wrote a book called *The World As I Found It*, I should have to include a report on my body, and should have to say which parts were subordinate to my will and which were not, etc., this being a way of isolating the subject, or rather of showing that in an important sense there is no subject; for it alone could *not* be mentioned in that book. –

Wait a minute. . . . Now, where did Wittgenstein go in this troubling statement? He disappears. Here while proposing to report on his life, Wittgenstein simultaneously seems to erase himself out of the picture.

You'll say he meant this purely philosophically, but for me it is a poet's song of origins and disappearances, of words and then word-covering silence.

Silence: Yes, it is very strange indeed for me to look back at this book four years later. But it's especially strange now as I try to finish another, very different novel; or perhaps I should say as it finishes me.

But, again, this old haven of mine, *The World As I Found It....* Flattening like a wave, the picture stills, and then, for better or worse, you, the author—you're out of that picture, that fictional space you've created. You're apart from it and, in a very real sense, you're quite irrelevant to it. The *I* is indeed another, and the subject remains forever elsewhere. This spent wave splashes and falls away, leaving me to wonder at its vanishing face—at what, or whom, I saw in this world that I left.

DAVID ST. JOHN

Café Rio

[ROPEWALK WRITERS' RETREAT]

Note: This talk was given at both the Port Townsend Writers' Conference in 1992 and the Ropewalk Writers' Retreat in 1993 in versions roughly approximate to this. It consists of radically edited sections of a book-length work in progress, entitled Mallarmé's Sailboat: American Poetry at the End of the Century. *What I try to do, in fairly obvious terms, is address some of the conditions, strengths, and dilemmas I think are facing American poets at this juncture in our history. Because of the editing, many of the felicities of the argument have been lost; I hope what follows doesn't come across as piecemeal. This edited pastiche from* Mallarmé's Sailboat *has its own title,* Café Rio, *and a premise I'll race through as quickly as possible.*

There is a primary speaker, a protagonist, who is remarkably like me, who perhaps, in fact, even is me. He has met in Paris a young couple just starting a café; the young woman, Solange, is a former painter who has studied in London at the Slade; the young man of the couple has survived the Yale English Department, the Harvard Divinity School, and three years as a chef for a Zen monastery in Zurich. His name is Zedediah, which after being shortened to his nickname, Zed, was corrupted by the zen monks into Brother Zero. After the prologue there is a scene and time shift. After a period of ten years, the speaker encounters the couple again after they've moved their café to, where else, my own neighborhood in Venice, California. The format is casual; conversations take place about many aspects of poetry. Because I've had to edit so severely, the biggest loss is the fuller sense of Solange and Brother Zero as sometimes unsympathetic interlocutors and as artistic figures in their own right. We begin then in Venice, with what is, I promise, the appearance of the only movie star in the whole essay.

One day I was sitting outside Café Rio with Brother Zero when a guy who
looked a lot like Mickey Rourke pulled up on his Harley. He was a regular, but it was unusual to see him so early in the day. He asked Zed for
some olive oil and when Zed brought it out he poured some into one
palm, rubbed his palms together, and then pushed both hands slowly
through the length of his hair until his hair gleamed in the sunlight just
like an anchovy. Whatta you guys doing, the quasi-Mickey asked. Well,
said Brother Zero, we were talking about poetry. The quasi-Mickey nodded. Bukowski's my man. In *Barfly* I could feel his poetic spirits overtake
me. I even started writing some poems myself. The maybe-Mickey ran
his hands through his hair once more, revved the engine on the Harley,
let out the clutch, and was gone. Wow, Zedediah said, turning to me, it
must feel very meaningful to be a poet in Los Angeles.

One afternoon Zedediah sat back in the kitchen reading Joseph Epstein's
article "Who Killed Poetry?" from an old issue of *Commentary*. He also
had on the table a piece Epstein referred to, Edmund Wilson's "Is Verse
a Dying Technique?" Brother Zero nodded as I came in and said, Everybody says poetry is dead or dying. They say that nobody reads poetry except poets and, therefore, that poetry has no rightful place in the cultural
life of our times. They say that we have to find a new popular audience
for poetry and that those to blame are the poets themselves, since in the
old days, of course, almost everybody read poetry, so it must be that now
poetry just doesn't relate to people the way it used to. But now listen to
this.
    He picked up a copy of the anthology *The Best American Poetry of 1989*
and began to read from the introduction by that volume's guest editor,
Donald Hall. He read:

Sixty years after Edmund Wilson told us that verse was dying, Joseph Epstein . . . reveals that it was murdered. Of course, Epstein's golden age – Stevens,
Frost, Williams – is Wilson's time of "demoralized weakness." Everything
changes and everything stays the same. Poetry was always in good shape twenty or
thirty years ago; *now* it has always gone to hell. I have heard this lamentation for
forty years, not only from distinguished critics and essayists, but from professors
and journalists who enjoy viewing our culture with alarm.

Zed paused, then reported that Joseph Epstein insisted in his article that, far from disliking poetry, he had been "taught that poetry was an exalted thing." Now, just listen to what Hall says about that, Zed continued:

> Worship is not love. People who at the age of fifty deplore the death of poetry are the same people who in their twenties were "taught to exalt it." The middle-aged poetry detractor is the student who hyperventilated at poetry readings thirty years earlier.... After college many people stop reading contemporary poetry. Why not? They become involved in journalism or scholarship, essay writing or editing, brokering or solid waste; they backslide from the undergraduate Church of Poetry. Years later, glancing belatedly at the poetic scene, they tell us that poetry is dead. They left poetry; therefore they blame poetry for leaving them. Really they lament their own aging. Don't we all? But some of us do not blame the poets.

Brother Zero put down the anthology and waited for me to say something. Don't forget, I told him, Donald Hall's irony and rancor have been well earned by a lifetime as an editor, poet, and literary chronicler. Yet he's one of our most eclectic readers of poetry, and as an editor and essayist, Donald Hall likes to reflect what he sees as the broad range of poetic styles and aesthetics in American poetry, one of the aspects, he believes, as do I, of its great strength. Look, I said, we live in a time of rich poetic diversity, both stylistically and culturally. But Hall can't help but feel disappointed at the fact that so many of these poetic branches of the American tree have become so fiercely isolated, self-congratulatory, and exclusionary. Whether the neoformalists (who, Hall points out, seem to have trouble scanning, as well as an alarming insensitivity to verbal music, neither a good sign in a formal poet), or the New Narrative poets, the language poets, the LA poets, the St. Marks poets, and so on, it doesn't matter—the point is that regionalism, parochialism, and provincialism result from these poetic "schools." In fact, these schools of poetry always serve the interests of the individual and the career, not of poetry itself. My own belief, I said to Zed, is that poets who run in packs are hungry for fame, not for inspiration.

Look, I said. Why can't we have all of our poets? Parochial perspectives lessen and cheapen our poetry. We all know that American poetry needs both Whitman's huge embrace and extended breath as well as the

precise lyric inscription of Dickinson. We've inherited the nostalgia for
transcendence along with what we're told is our poetic responsibility to
the "real." We have to make a reckoning with both, otherwise these
weights are capable of drowning us all.

Brother Zero asked, What about you? Tell us what you think about poetry in traditional forms. You know, rhymes and meter? I can't figure out
why you use meters and rhymes in some of your poems but not others.
What's up? It's simple, I said. It just depends on the poem; you can't be
programmatic about it. Even the strictest formal urge still has to feel or-
ganic and proper to the poem. Frank O'Hara once said, "As for measure
and other technical apparatus, that's just common sense: if you're going
to buy a pair of pants you want them to be tight enough so everyone will
want to go to bed with you." And Wallace Stevens said that a poet's sense
of form is simply a matter of one's own nervous system. It's partly craft,
partly the pressure of the language, and partly the poem's own sense of
movement. A poet always has to listen. Sometimes the poem's shape arrives in the imagination just like desire. Sometimes you're in the back-
seat of a '58 Impala and sometimes you're at La Tour D'Argent. You and
the poem either behave accordingly, or you let your inappropriate behavior help provide some of the poem's tension, drive, and excitement. It's
all in the poem's enactment.

   I think I get it, said Brother Zero. Duck burgers and Dion at La Tour
D'Argent.

I'd just sat down to my cappuccino one morning when Zed came over and
whispered in my ear, "The poet is the priest of the invisible." I know, I
said, but who told you. Zed looked out across the beach toward the Pacific. Wallace Stevens, he whispered again. Yeah, I said. Me too. Solange
pulled a tray of croissants out of the oven. Jesus, she said. I really hate it
when men get vatic.

I was trying to explain to Solange what I thought a poem was. Sometimes
it's easier to say what a poem isn't, I began. It isn't linear. "Prose pro-
ceeds; verse reverses," I told her, quoting Richard Howard paraphrasing
Valéry. Often, we have to read a poem the way we "read" a painting or a
passage of cinema, because of the materiality of the language and the el-

liptical nature of its movements. A contemporary poem often uses the grammar of film, exploiting those elliptical movements that suggest rather than delineate narrative. In their workings, poems are perhaps most of all like mobiles, each part casting light on every other part as the whole poem turns slowly within the voice of its speaker.

Solange looked up from her buttered croissant. Mobiles? she asked. I ignored her. We live in a world fixed by its names, a world that's often imprisoned by the inadequacy of those names, both the names for the world we've inherited and the names we ourselves have imposed. Poems and poets want to help free us from those fixed perspectives; they want to allow us to see the world anew, with the freshness and awe it deserves. A poet has to engage in a kind of unnaming, before the poem's renaming of the world can begin. And in a world in which language is often reduced to a kind of white noise, poetry is one of the few sanctuaries we can turn to in order to experience language being used with integrity, precision, power, and beauty.

Poetry is about verbal enactment, I went on. It's the drama of the self and the self's dispersal into language, of the consciousness of the self-consciousness of consciousness, played out on the stage of language. The poem is not an object, not something flat and two-dimensional, bound or pressed like a leaf between the pages of an anthology; a poem is an experience. Poetry, and all art for that matter, has the dramatic ability to introduce us to, and to produce within us, unfamiliar modes and aspects of perception – as well as alternative models and constructs of consciousness and understanding.

Think of poems as small models of consciousness; in their enactments they offer us a variety of architectures of perception that may be completely unfamiliar to us. Even if those models of perception seem at first disturbing, or even threatening, as we absorb them and allow them entry into our own experience, the experience of reading, they become part of the vocabulary of our understanding of the world. Once more: A poem or any work of art is an *experience*, not simply an object to be considered, admired, regarded, explicated, revered . . . and dismissed.

Art makes possible the future. Art doesn't simply reflect the conditions and complexities of its own time; art also tries to anticipate and to create new structures of experience. Marcuse said it: Art shatters everyday experience and anticipates a different reality principle.

Not only can art disrupt the imprisoning surface of the quotidian, making possible the reinvention of the daily into the "new," art also recognizes the ways in which our present understandings, assumptions, and perceptions about ourselves, in both artistic and cultural terms, are doomed to inadequacy; and art must posit the new alternative constructs of understanding and perception.

Solange had finished her croissant; as she looked up at me, I could see she still had a little tear of butter sliding along her chin like a tiny yellow toboggan. I reached across the table and interrupted its course.

OK, I said. Let's try going at it this way. Think how many of the lessons of the twentieth century have been the lessons of fragmentation and disjunction; as our experience itself seems to have accelerated, we've been faced with a truly kaleidoscopic display. In a single day, we're faced with a breathtaking variety of events and experiences; and though our experience may be disjunctive and fragmentary, our experiencing *of* these events must remain necessarily fluid, or else that sense of fragmentation and breakdown, which is external, will be taken in to become our own.

One of the things that poetry allows us is a way to understand how these jagged, fragmented, and potentially damaging pieces of experience that make up our lives can be held and supported by what is fluid and fluent in consciousness. It's the act of the mind, as Stevens called it in his poem "Of Modern Poetry," as it experiences the event of the poem that allows us to bring these new architectures of experience into our lives and poetic vocabularies.

One night I confessed to Solange and Zed that I was writing a book I wanted to title *Mallarmé's Sailboat*. When they asked why that title, I deferred the question and said, instead, let me read you something. I pulled out an essay not by a poet, but by one of the great masters of contemporary fiction, Donald Barthelme. In the essay, called "Not Knowing," Bartheleme is meditating on modern art, the fiction of those, including himself, he calls "alleged Postmodernists," as well as the nature and conditions of language. Barthelme turns to one of his own heroes of literature, Stéphane Mallarmé. He says:

With Mallarmé the effort toward mimesis, the representation of the external world, becomes a much more complex thing than it had been previously. Mallarmé shakes words loose from their attachments and bestows new meanings upon them, meanings which point not toward the external world but towards the Absolute, acts of poetic intuition. This is a fateful step; not for nothing does [Roland] Barthes call him the Hamlet of literature. It produces, for one thing, a poetry of unprecedented difficulty. You will find no Mallarmé in Bartlett's *Familiar Quotations*. . . . Mallarmé's work is also, and perhaps most importantly, a step toward establishing a new ontological status for the poem, as an object in the world rather than a representation of the world. But the ground seized is dangerous ground. After Mallarmé the struggle to renew language becomes a given for the writer, his exemplary quest an imperative. Mallarmé's work, "This whisper that is so close to silence," as Marcel Raymond calls it, is at once a liberation and a loss to silence of a great deal of territory.

Barthelme adds, near the end of his essay, "Art is a true account of the activity of the mind. Because consciousness, in Husserl's formation, is always consciousness *of* something, art thinks ever of the world, cannot not think of the world, could not turn its back on the world even if it wished to."

For Barthelme as well as for Mallarmé, as well as for Wallace Stevens, it is this clearly dangerous yet potentially revelatory alchemical mixture of language with the world (or as Stevens would formulate it, the imagination mediated by the pressures of reality) that produces contemporary artistic process. Poets are always at work forging those architectures of language that will make it possible for us, as well as for readers to come, to inhabit a world we are only beginning to imagine.

Brother Zero opened another bottle of his favorite Antinori Chianti Reserva and I held out my glass. If what you've been saying is really true, he said, then why, in American poetry, is that love of the sensuality of language and the complexity of poetic process you keep talking about so hard to find?

First of all, I said, American poetry distrusts eloquence. From the moment that Puritan plain style took hold, we've struggled with our feelings about complex and beautiful language. Americans seem to believe that ambiguity and complexity in language constitute a kind of moral failure.

We've always equated sincerity and integrity with simplicity in language, and regarded eloquence as the suspicious achievement of the foreigner or the city slicker. If pleasure and play in life are the Devil's toolbox, then pleasure and play in language are the Devil's tongue.

We honor and prize that oaklike solidity of the farmer and the cowboy. Not real farmers and cowboys (who'll often talk your ear off telling rich and extraordinary stories). I mean our mythology of them – the mythology of their profound reticence. The taciturn New England farmer and the laconic Western cowboy are our national models. Their linguistic discretion, we feel, is so profound that it must border on great wisdom. We're enthralled when, in the face of great danger, tension, and even the cascading emotions of true love, our hero can step forward with a monosyllabic reply. Our hero doesn't say more than he has to, and he says it plain. For Americans who mistrust those who can manipulate language, the ideal verbal hero is Gary Cooper. American poetry has become the Gary Cooper school of poetry.*

It would be tempting to say this is a rural matter, to say that these prejudices about language are a class matter, or a regional phenomenon; but that isn't true. For one thing, these profound suspicions have led us to elect and revere at least one recent president whose vocabulary of public discourse purposely did not exceed that of an average five-year-old. As an actor, a former actor in Westerns no less, Ronald Reagan understood the great need in the American heart to believe that what we were being told was the truth, and that the truth was, as every American knows, always something very simple. The world might try to tell us that it is a complicated, subtle, and complex place, but Reagan knew that *we* knew better than that – that the truth is never a complicated thing. The genius of Ronald Reagan and his handlers was that they saw so clearly that the Cooperesque Reagan didn't really have to say or explain anything. To do that, in fact, would be absolutely contrary to what the public wanted. The lie of simplicity, the strategy of the reductive.

It is a lie and a strategy that, I believe, infects much of American poetry. We can't pick up a contemporary poem without being stunned by the flatness of its diction and its affect of simplicity. This fear of verbal beauty, this terror of ambiguity, has dictated a poetry that uses as its

*A phrase first coined by Henri Coulette.

cover the ideal of the conversational. But this is not what William Carlos Williams had in mind when he called for a poetry of an American vernacular; this is not what Williams hoped for in asking for a poetry that resembled speech. Williams assumed that there would remain a faith in verbal complexities that have instead become equated with deception (in the public arena) and with high-art elitisms (in the poetic arena). Williams's love of the American voice has been misunderstood as a love of the ordinary in language. Certainly Williams and Stevens both loved the "ordinary," the quotidian, but the ordinary as it was transformed by language.

We can love the democratic ideal in the expansiveness of Whitman's gestures; we can love the stark and sometimes telegraphic utterances of Robert Creeley, or the handmade, stone-by-stone, delicately cobbled poems of Gary Snyder; we can love them all without sacrificing a love of complex, internal poetic architectures and our thrill in the texture and dimension of their language.

We've reached a state in our poetry where the prevailing mode is often one of reportage. The more documentary the poem, the more genuine it must therefore be. This is a dangerous and truly reactionary force in our poetry. It imagines that poetry is to be objectified, that a poem is noted with approval or disapproval in relation to an integrity that is based on the documentary force of the poem's content.

This means the most powerful transformative potential of poetry, the power of poetic enactment to engage a reader in sympathies, empathies, and experiences that otherwise would be outside of the reader's realm, will begin to be seen as an irrelevant aspect of our poetry. The poetry of reportage is a poetry of smugness, self-satisfaction, and self-congratulaton; it is a poetry that is dedicated to the elevation and the celebration of the most banal aspects of the self.

For me, it has been astonishing to watch how some American poetry has looked to the notion of a poetry of witness, as exemplified by both Eastern European and South American poets, and then reduced the fierce ethical and moral vision of those attempts to a maudlin rendering of daily narrative. The political meditations of some of these American poets — which are both ahistorical and highly personalized — strike me as both parasitical and parroting; they have appropriated a poetic response that was the result of a true political urgency and the urgency of personal conscience and they have attempted to weld it onto a poetry of self-exposition.

When we read one of these poems, we are expected to be awed by both the sensitivity of the poet and the depth of his or her convictions, political or otherwise. Why, it is perfectly fair to ask, do I feel these poems are so reactionary? Because they exist as notations of the cultural and political voyeur; and more importantly, they offer absolutely no transformative enactment for a reader, the event that I believe is the true possibility in a poem seeking a political effect. The message is not enough. The experience of the conditions of the message is everything. In writing classes we say show, don't tell. But here even the "showing" is a cheat; unless a poem verbally enacts its model of consciousness in a way that allows for this recognition by and transformation of the reader, then the poem remains an object of cultural, emotional, and political voyeurism. The poverty of language has always had political implications. Our aesthetic of reduction is in danger of becoming an aesthetic of depletion; it's time for a poetics of plenitude, for the utility now of the sensual and the beautiful.

Edited out here is a discussion, in rapid-fire succession, of style, beauty, and the place of mystery in poetry. This discussion of mystery leads to a digression on the poetic mask, which itself becomes entirely too oracular for the speaker's own good. In any case:

By this time, Solange was bathing my forehead with wet towels and Brother Zero was feeding me steamed and buttered snails he was pulling delicately from their shells. It was like being backstage at Delphi. I had no idea what I had been saying, but Solange and Brother Zero had taken off all of their jewelry and placed it before me on a gorgeous Limoges plate. They knew the only appetite I had at that moment was for what the physical world had found to be both luminous and irreducible.

The next morning Brother Zero brought out an espresso and asked: If, in poetry, the element of *time* includes desire, death, and all aspects of passage, then tell me about *silence*. Silence, said Solange, joining us, is the ground against which every poem is figured; silence is the angel that wishes to wrestle each poet to both that and the literal ground. Solange and Zedediah looked at me; I didn't know what to say, what to add. The question had somehow left me exhausted and distracted. I decided to tell them the story of Mallarmé's sailboat, as it had a kind of zen resonance I knew they would both admire. This is how the story goes:

Julie Manet was the daughter of the wonderful painter Berthe Morisot and Eugène Manet, brother of Edouard. Julie Manet grew up in a household frequented by both writers and painters—Degas, Renoir, Monet, and one of her family's very closest friends, Mallarmé. The Manet family often visited with the Mallarmé family, both in Paris and at their respective summer homes along the Seine. Julie Manet and Mallarmé's daughter, Geneviève, became close friends. Mallarmé himself loved to stay each summer near the village of Valvins, where he could sail his beloved sailboat. Sometimes both Morisot and Julie would accompany Mallarmé, and both mother and daughter painted exquisite and delicate canvases of Mallarmé alone out in his sailboat.

In 1893, a year after the death of her father, Eugène, Julie Manet began a diary; she was not quite fifteen years old. Berthe Morisot, after the death of her husband, sensing the fragility of her own health, named as guardian for her daughter her most trusted friend, Mallarmé. In 1895, Berthe Morisot also died, and Mallarmé became an even more central figure in the life of young Julie. Three years later, in September of 1898, without warning, Mallarmé himself died. Though devastated, Julie Manet devoted herself to trying to console Geneviève and Madame Mallarmé. The following is a part of the entry from Julie Manet's diary for Sunday, September 11, 1898, the day of Mallarmé's funeral. The boat mentioned is, of course, Mallarmé's sailboat.

> We arrived at Valvins about 2 o'clock. How dreadful it was to go down the path beside the Seine toward the small country place when we couldn't help thinking that the person for whom we were shedding tears wasn't there anymore. The boat seemed to be quite solitary—his boat, the boat that he liked so much—and it reminded me of a first outing in it in '87 with Maman and Papa, who asked Mr. Mallarmé if he had ever written anything about his boat. "No," he replied, casting a glance at its sail, "for once, I am leaving this great page blank."

ALAN CHEUSE

Writing It Down for James: Some Thoughts on Reading toward the Millennium

[PORT TOWNSEND WRITERS' CONFERENCE]

On a cold rainy Washington night several Decembers back this traveler drove over to the Congressional Office Building on Capitol Hill to attend the Christmas party of a local literacy council. A group of young professionals, many of them lawyers and college teachers, who serve as tutors for the District's largest adult literacy project – not an official part of either the D.C. or the federal government but rather a nonprofit organization that belongs to a national umbrella group that fosters the teaching of reading to adults – served plates of roast turkey and baked ham and many side dishes to a couple of dozen adults and a few teenagers, almost all of them black, who all share the desire to learn how to read.

One of these late bloomers was a fifty-three-year-old truck driver from South Carolina named James. James picked up a newspaper only about a year and a half ago after a lifetime of work and raising a family. He had dropped out of school at the age of six to pick crops at nearby farms and never went back. Though unable to read a word, he'd worked as a stevedore and as a foreman at a shipping company, and for the last two decades has been working as a teamster, in some instances hauling his load as far as the Canadian border without knowing how to read the road signs.

When I expressed my astonishment at this feat, James laughed and said, "Hey, once you pass the driver's test, the rest ain't all that hard. It's usually just a matter of counting. Counting the stop signs, things like that. You recognize landmarks in town or out on the road and you sort of steer by them."

But after a lifetime of living in his own country as though it were a foreign land where he didn't know the language, James decided that since all his children had learned to read and gone on to good jobs, he could take the time out to learn how to read himself. This he told me over a plate of food, his right leg moving up and down, up and down, his plate shaking on his lap.

"I wanted to learn to read a newspaper, see? I wanted to *read* about life, not just live it. So I can just about do that now. And now I want to read a whole book. I want to read a story. A good story."

The desire for a good story – that had been on my own mind ever since I could remember. And for the last three decades, reading – and writing – had become a large portion of my daily life. I write, usually, into the early afternoon, and the rest of the day, when I'm not leading a workshop or at the gym or at the supermarket or the movies, I give over to reading. Read, read, read, a rage to read. It's an appetite as great as that for sex or food or even for the air we breathe. Death will be a great disappointment if there is no love or family or friends that come with it, but I'd even forgo food in the next life (if there is one) if I could go on reading the good new novels as they come out. In the last ten years I've reviewed nearly five hundred books for National Public Radio's evening newsmagazine *All Things Considered,* and like most people who love narrative, whether fiction or history or politics or science (though fiction is the best narrative of them all), I've read a lot more than those I've reviewed during this past decade, rereading books as I teach them to my writing students (because as I explain to them, thinking at the same time that if I have to explain it to them then perhaps they are already lost, good writers are good readers and great writers are great readers), rereading as I write essays and articles as well as reviews.

But a lifetime – yours, mine – with books has to begin somewhere. And while talking with James over our plates of turkey at the literacy party, I kept on trying to recall exactly when it was I first learned how to read. James could pinpoint his own beginning with the printed word. On a certain night in June in Washington at a restaurant where he had first met his tutor. Before that time, the printed language was a mystery to him, a cipher used by the rest of the world to keep him constantly on his toes. On the job he devised elaborate formulas to keep up with his work. In the supermarket he often depended on the kindness of strangers to tell him where certain foods were located. And as he was talking about his own preliterate life as an adult, I got carried back to one of the few preliterate scenes in my own memory.

Once upon a time a young boy – he must have been about three years old – crawled into bed with his mother and father. It was a Sunday morning, in spring, probably, because even though it was light outside the window, his father still lay in bed rather than having gone to work. While his mother created a space between them where the boy might burrow beneath the covers, his father reached over to the night table and picked up a rectangular object about six inches by nine inches – it had an orange and sepia cover, an abstract design that suggested not-quite-formed stars and crescents – that he said he had just found in his old trunk from a place he called *Roosh*-a. The boy loved the sound of the word and asked his father to say it again: *Roosh*-a. There was a smell to the object, too, this thing made of paper and bound in stiff board, the odor of dust and oranges that had been lying long in the hot sun.

When his father opened the front of it, the boy noticed strange designs stretched out in rows. The only thing he recognized was a drawing, that of a golden roosterlike bird. "The Tale of the Golden Cockerel," his father announced as he fixed his eye on the page and began to speak in a strange and incomprehensible fashion, making a series of globlike and skidding sounds, with a lot of phushes and ticks and bubblelike slurs and pauses.

The boy was me, of course, and the man was my father reading to me in Russian, a language I've never learned, from a book of fairy tales that has long ago been lost in the flood of years that rushes through a family's life. And he of course is gone, too, and I'm old enough now to have a while ago put aside such fairy tales and think instead about what novels to give as gifts to my children for Christmas and other occasions. But I still recall the way my father opened to the first page of that now lost volume and began to make those sounds with his mouth and tongue, interpreting the odd designs in front of him as if it were the easiest thing in the world. It was from this day on that I decided, I believe – if "deciding" is what children at that age ever do – that I would learn to read for myself.

I don't actually remember when I first mastered this basic intellectual aptitude. As Roger Shattuck has pointed out in a recent essay, few of us do. "Most minds," he says, "bury those early faltering steps under recollections of later rewards – the fairy tales or comic books on which we perfected our new skill." But some writers have tried to remember. Novelist Nicholas Delbanco describes a wonderful example of this when he writes of a transatlantic crossing, from England to America, at the age of six. On the third day out, he recalls, he received his first pair of long pants and he taught himself to read using a book about boats. Suddenly "the alphabet's tumblers went 'click,' I remember the feel of it, the pride in it, the pleasure, the way the world made sense." Only as a middle-aged adult did he find a copy of a book called "Henry's Green Wagon" inscribed to him from his kindergarten teacher in London for being "the best reader in Miss Jamaica's Kindergarten Class" in the year before his voyage.

I don't recollect, beyond my one tantalizing session with the book of Russian fairy tales, that my father ever read to me again. Or my mother. Though I suppose they must have. I certainly hope that my children recall the times that I read to them. If Delbanco can't recall winning his award from Miss Jamaica's kindergarten class I probably shouldn't expect my son or daughters to keep in mind the hours we spent going over "The Little Engine That Could" or the "Ant and Bee" stories. If we do teach our children to read we can never forget the first few times that they skate off across the page on their own, a thrill in life that resembles something like the first time we sped away on our bikes without the use of training wheels.

An industry now supports this hope-filled activity. The middle class is urged to prep its children in advance of school. "Improved reading skills begin at home," says a headline in the "Parent and Child" column of the *New York Times*. You can buy books, take courses. And you can hook your child up to your computer and plug in such programs as the Disney-made "Mickey's ABCs" and "Follow the Reader." You can learn tips about how to encourage your children to read. And read to them yourself. In a statement of what seems to be the original sin of illiteracy, Dr. Michael Pressley, a professor of educational psychology at the University of Maryland, is quoted as saying that "the kids who have the most trouble tend to have parents who didn't read to them when they were younger... and didn't see their parents or other people reading and writing."

But just as I have only that single memory of being read to, and in Russian besides, I don't recall seeing my parents read much at all. I do have the faint recollection of watching my father sit in a small alcove of a second-floor apartment on lower State Street in Perth Amboy, New Jersey, tapping on the keys of a small black typewriter, trying to write stories in English in the manner of the Russian satirists Ilf and Petrov. But I never saw him read anything other than the newspaper or a beat-up old copy of Richard Halliburton's *The Nine Wonders of the World*, the texture of whose cover and quality of whose photographs – waterfalls, drawings of statues – I recall rather than any text. My mother might have read the front page of the newspaper. I never saw her hold any book in her hand.

But I grew up reading, reading like a bandit. And no fairy tales for me. I went straight to comic books, *Archie* comics at first, and then the superheroes, *Superman* and *Batman*, *Plastic Man*, *Wonder Woman*, and then on to the horror comics, *EC Stories*, and *The Heap*, building a collection that rivaled just about any in the neighborhood. Of a Saturday you could see us comics fans, pushing baby carriages (left over from our younger siblings' infancies) filled with our collections on our way to trade meets at someone's house. After a while a quest for something more than *Archie* and so forth sent me onward to better reading, which meant, of course, *Classics Illustrated*. The western world's greatest poems and stories turned into comic books, from the *Iliad* and *Odyssey* on through the centuries all the way to Poe: that was my reading for the years of early adolescence.

Some educators these days are encouraging parents to allow their kids to cut their first reading teeth on *Classics Illustrated*, then watch them go on to more complicated books. I watched myself graduate to the serialized Christmas story that appeared in our local newspaper each December, and then to the sea adventures of C. S. Forester, his Captain Horatio Hornblower series, to years and years of science fiction novels and short stories. Although we "read" *Silas Marner* in junior high school I don't remember a thing about it. It was always the adventure stories and speculative fiction that captured me.

Marcel Proust's fictional Marcel writes of his afternoons with novels in the fabled Combray:

On the sort of screen dappled with different states and impressions which my consciousness would simultaneously unfold while I was reading, my innermost impulse, the lever whose incessant movements controlled everything else, was my belief in the philosophic richness and beauty of the book I was reading, and my desire to appropriate them for myself, whatever the book might be. . . . Next to this central belief which, while I was reading, would be constantly reaching out from my inner self to the outer world, towards the discovery of truth, came the emotions roused in me by the action in which I was taking part, for these afternoons were crammed with more dramatic events than occur, often, in a whole lifetime. These were the events taking place in the book I was reading. . . .

How many summer afternoons and long winter evenings this Jersey Marcel, yours truly, spent lost in this fashion! As you all have been lost, discovering and deepening your imaginative life in such a way as to change your ordinary waking physical life forever.

Except for those math geniuses who are probably anomalies when it comes to the quality of their minds, most of us find this period in which we encounter the mental adventures of reading the most important part of our maturation. Though to try and watch it happen is to see nothing. Last spring, for example, I spent a few days behind one-way glass observing an eighth-grade reading class at a middle school in Huntsville, Texas. I'm not sure what I expected to find, but this was what I saw. Several dozen kids from ages eleven to thirteen seated at their desks or sprawled on large cushions on the floor holding books open in front of them. They moved their limbs and twitched their eyes as they might have in sleep. Scarcely any of them did more than change position on the cushions or cross or extend their legs beneath their desks. Yet the internal processes in their minds, no more visible than coal changing under pressure into diamond, would change their lives. It will help them discover the world in a way like no other; to learn of history and philosophy and science and art; to acquire an awareness of God and insects, of water and the nature of life in a mining town in Belgium in 1900; to study Buddhism and physics, or merely to keep boredom at arm's length on an autumn evening in Great Falls, Montana; to become army captains and sales managers and priests and cotton farmers; and to ponder, if they are so inclined, the relation between their hometown, in this case, Huntsville, Texas, and the rest of the state, the country, the continent, the world, the solar system, galaxy, and cosmos.

However, you have only to observe a lower-level reading class in order to be reminded, if you need such an elemental tip, that this skill is not part of what we would call human nature. Kids study the shape of the letters and learn to sound each letter, group of letters, then make words. We've sounded letters, vowels and consonants resounding and popping, for our own kids. To watch a whole batch of them at once get this training is like witnessing the first hatching of tree frogs in a warm climate in early spring. The entire air fairly sings and squeaks with the wondering noise of it all. But despite the illusion of the naturalness of reading, an activity as everyday as breathing, this skill is, in the history of Western culture, a relatively new invention. For the majority of humanity in Europe and the West, verbal art was spoken or sung. And what we now call illiteracy was once the normal condition of culture in what we also name as the Golden Age of Greece.

The thousand years or more prior to sixth-century-B.C. Athens was the time of the Homeric rhetors or rhapsodes, who chanted and sang the great poems of the culture to devoted audiences. It was only with the faltering of the Homeric tradition, when it seemed as though the transmission of the poems in memory from one generation to the next was in danger of dying out, that Pisistratus, the Greek tyrant, ordered that scribes record the performance of the two great epics, the *Iliad* and the *Odyssey*, on papyrus lest they be lost for all time.

Maybe that's when paradise was truly lost, when it became necessary to read the great songs that had formerly been sung. Is it E. M. Cioran who describes this transition as the culture's "fall into language"? Prior to this time no one read because there was no written language, but a hunger was present, present, it seems, from the beginnings of human culture, the hunger for story, for narrative, for the arrangement of incidents into an action both pleasing and instructional, perhaps even an action that might move the listener to feel pity and fear. This craving for order with emotional resonance was satisfied during the pre-Classical period in the Mediterranean by oral epic only.

Drama arose during the fifth century B.C. and filled, among its other functions, the traditional need for a public gathering at which poetry was performed over an extended period of time. But by the first century A.D., poetry and drama were read more often on papyrus then performed. Prose narratives were composed as well, but these, like the *Satyricon*, seemed to take second place to the more engaging works of history in the mind of an audience looking, apparently, both for a way to restore a certain order to a life from which the formerly awesome power of the old gods had faded and for exciting and interesting stories that spoke to their own daily round.

Between the decline of Greece and Rome and the withering away of the Christendom that arose to take their place, most Westerners had to settle for one book, the Bible, with its multitude of stories, as the storehouse of narrative. It wasn't really until the fourteenth century and the creation of *The Decameron* that secular stories came to prominence as literary art—folk narratives were as plentiful as trees—in Europe. As every schoolkid used to know, the invention of movable type eventually made possible the wide dissemination of texts of all varieties, not just the Bible, for which the printing press was first widely used. After Luther's revolt against Rome's authority as the prime interpreter of the Holy Book, literacy became a necessity in his part of Europe for the religious. Soon it evolved into a means of power among the rising merchant class, and reading became a sign that a person was wholly civilized.

Consider for a moment what this meant in existential terms for the inhabitants of European society. In the great Homeric age of Greece, any citizen of Athens who could attend the performances of the epics—at four seasonal renderings each year in the great amphitheater of the city—could apprehend them merely by listening attentively. To be a citizen thus meant among other things to be a listener, collectively, with all the other citizens of Athens. You listened and the words of the gods, by means of the conduit of the poet, went directly to your ears, telling of the great heroes and heroines, gods and goddesses, engaged in the straightening out, or messing up, of epic affairs in heaven, earth, and the underworld.

With the breakup of this oral culture and the rise of scriptural authority, reading became a prized activity, not just for the priesthood but for the elite of the Continent's court and fief. The book became a metaphor for the world, and reading emerged as a method for interpreting God's creation. To be illiterate meant one stood several stages removed from a knowledge of sacred reality. The idea that one listens to the words of the epic poet and thus hears the language of the Muses directly in one's ears becomes, in this thousand-year interregnum between the demise of oral poetry and the establishment of a secular reading culture, static and sterile when the priest, rather than the poet, serves as conduit between holy work and worshiper. With the secularization of storytelling, from Boccaccio forward, the printed word became even further detached from its origins in sacred poetry, telling stories of the death of kings and then barons and then squires so that by the time of Balzac, say, readers learned of the lives, loves, and sorrows of the denizens of a great secular city, which is to say, themselves.

As the story evolves – some might want to say descends – from Scripture to secular tales of middle-class life, the relation of text to reader evolves as well. Christian theology demanded a singular oath from its worshipers, the acceptance of Christ as a personal savior. Eighteen hundred years later the individual picks up a copy of *Tom Jones* and finds that the story illuminates part of his or her daily round, a far cry from any hint of salvation. In fact, quite the opposite, if you consider the distance between the hope of heaven and the worlds in contemporary fiction. To pass one's eyes across the lines of the Holy Writ was an act of prayer. What is it then to read modern fiction?

Proust's Marcel has – again – a pretty good way of seeing it. A real person, he asserts, because he is known to us only through our senses, remains opaque to us.

If some misfortune comes to him, it is only in one small section of the complete idea we have of him that we are capable of feeling any emotion; indeed it is only in one small section of the complete idea he has of himself that he is capable of feeling any emotion either. The novelist's happy discovery was to think of substituting for those opaque sections, impenetrable to the human soul, their equivalent in immaterial sections, things, that is, which one's soul can assimilate. After which it matters not that the actions, the feelings of this new order of creatures appears to us in the guise of truth, since we have made them our own, since it is in ourselves that they are happening, that they are holding in thrall, as we feverishly turn over the pages of the book, our quickened breath and staring eyes. And once the novelist has brought us to this state, in which, as in all purely mental states, every emotion is multiplied tenfold, into which his book comes to disturb us as might a dream, but a dream more lucid and more abiding than those which come to us in sleep, why then, for the space of an hour he sets free within us all the joys and sorrows in the world, a few of which only we should have to spend years of our actual life in getting to know, and the most intense of which would never be revealed to us because the slow course of their development prevents us from perceiving them.

So we read for pleasure? And for a glimpse of what a coherent vision of the world might be like? It may well be that putting together in our own minds a lifetime of novel-reading is as close to knowing what it must be like in the mind of God. From these simple stories, of a foolish hidalgo in search of a phantom lover, of the way the past rises up against the present in an English village called Middlemarch, of a Jewish advertising salesman wandering about Dublin looking for sympathy, of a Mississippi family plagued by alcoholism, madness, and imagined incest, of a woman named Maria who aimlessly drives the LA freeways, we make up a cosmos.

Think of reading then as an act of praise – of prayer, even – in which the individual reasserts his or her devotion to creation and to the immanent world in which we reside, a world in which every aspect of life, from old used tires piled high in a trash heap to the multiform patterns of snowflakes on a day in high winter, from the sickness of murder to the charity of parenthood, all make up part of a larger pattern. And when we read, we reenact that pattern, an activity that may be as close to serious prayer as most of us will get. Or want to. The modern organized religions hold no patent on expressing devotion to the universe. In fact, the pagan poets, the epic Homers of the oldest stories of the western Mediterranean, show a lot more imagination when it comes to creating great characters and overarching plots than the lyricists and lamenters of the Old and New Testaments. Some great poetry in the former, but nothing much in the latter unless you're spiritually bound to the text. Apply the test of narrative coherence, and the pagan epics win hands down. And if the response of the reader, the immersion into a story that delights and instructs in the deepest fashion we know, is any test of the presence of godliness, there's no doubt in my mind which stories show the mark of real deity.

If there is such a thing. The great hype about our present epoch is that we've moved into a period of technology with exponential possibility. The computer has become the metaphor for God. Fine with me. I'm an old science fiction fan from way back when I first started reading. Let's fly to Jupiter, let's shine our penlights into black holes. But on those long flights to the outer planets, or hyperspace journeys between galaxies, there's going to be time that's free. Maybe some techno-hotshots will want to use those hours, or months, or years, to play computer games or speak with voice-activated viewer-integrated videos. But most of the crew and/or passengers will probably want to read. And what will we do with our spare time once we move out beyond this current pioneering age of space exploration?

Imagine an engineer lying in his bunk in a space station at the outer reaches of our solar system with a peerless view of stars, to borrow a phrase, like dust. As people such as this have done for – what's the phrase here? – countless eons, he picks up a copy of a book, or punches out the title on his computer screen, and begins to read, or, if you will, scan the text. And what might it be? Anything from the stories of Louis L'Amour to *Paradise Lost* to *Moby Dick*, no doubt. Consider how the poetry of Milton or the ocean scenes of Melville or the cowpokes and bandits of L'Amour would carry him back to Earth themes and Earth places. Even if he's never set foot on Earth, these are still the stories of the species' home place.

Reading – reading is home itself, the place where we go when we wish to be with ourselves and our own minds and our own hearts. It is an act of the eye which, unlike the viewing of painting or film, has little to do with what the eye perceives before it. Theater and film are the imagination externalized, the created images of the minds of other parties performed objectively before us. While viewing a dance or a play, our eye is captive. Narrative prose and poetry, like music, represent a different and, I believe, higher form of representation. The words, like musical notations, are mere potential art, waiting to be performed by the reader on the interior stage of the imagination. And just as nothing could be more public than the performance of a play, nothing could be more private than reading a novel or story. As novelist Laura Furman recently suggested, reading may in fact be the last private activity of merit in our culture.

Neurologically one can distinguish the act of reading from the perception of other art forms, such as dance and drama, and one can see how it has a social reality distinct from the external performance, and perception, of ancient oral poetry, medieval drama, and all the other theatrical and visual art that has come after. Unlike oral poetry, which presumed the presence of a community ethos and the absence of what we would call individual ego, prose on the page demands individual participation and, ever since the advent of the age of symbolism, individual interpretation. Everyone in the Homeric audience understood the explicit meaning of the poems – there were no implicit meanings – and celebrated these values and beliefs by means of listening. Since the middle of the eighteenth century, readers have pondered the implicit values of a work within the confines of their own imaginations, and sometimes despaired of a world in which such solitariness is the norm and values are determined by the situation of the individual.

It's no wonder then that we all know so many people who never dare venture seriously into the world of reading. For most people a functioning imagination can be a treacherous and even frightening possession, generating trivial but annoying conditions such as hypochondria, on the one hand, and much more dangerous situations such as jealousy, paranoia, and megalomania on the other. In this regard, we read *Don Quixote*, the first modern novel, as a book about the dangers of taking books literally. Logos detached from its divine origins is a symbol awaiting interpretation by the god within us, which is to say, our imaginative powers. Woe to him – look at poor Quixote – who takes it at face value.

But that woe, the woe of literalism in an age of symbolic interpretation, is exactly what many Americans rush to embrace, cheered on by McLuhanite theoreticians of the new media. The flat screen, the so-called interactive game, has become the new repository for the faith of tens of millions, the perfect altar for our neo-Puritanical faith in which efficacy is next to godliness, and poetry (as Auden puts it in his elegy for Yeats) "makes nothing happen," and fiction is relegated to the dustbin of the new age. There seem to be two kinds of citizens in this nation that produced *Moby Dick*, either Ahabs or Ishmaels, and the former appear to be growing in direct proportion to the growth in population while the latter may be diminishing in number.

The figures on readership in America and the reading aptitude scores seem to suggest that this is so. More Ahabs, fewer Ishmaels. American students are reading less and less and watching more and more television every year. The majority of American students, it seems, read only to get along, most of them having been taken over by the games mentality of the new high-tech sales culture. So-called computer literacy has led to what we can only hope is a temporary rise in a new variety of illiteracy, the willful avoidance of narrative fiction and poetry as a means of knowledge and awareness. For the new exploding ranks of American students it seems to be Gameboy over C. S. Forester, and coming right up behind Gameboy, and as far and away from computer games today as they are from pinball, is the burgeoning new industry of virtual reality or VR. Probably within the next five years and certainly within the next ten, VR will become the distraction of choice for the majority of schoolkids and reading will be demoted even further down the line than where it is now, somewhere between violin lessons and learning a foreign language. In other words, it will become an activity for the few and elite, just as it was in Goethe's Germany, where out of sixty million inhabitants only about sixty thousand could read.

That's one scenario, anyway, and not an impossible one, considering the current state of popular culture in which trash seems to have driven out the good. From Emerson to Donahue, from Twain to Fulghum, it's been a bad long slide downward. There are some areas, of course, where we can see actual evolutionary forces at work to good ends, particularly in music. When you consider the way in which jazz has worked its way into the majority consciousness – and radio programming – or the rise of blue- grass, there's cause for celebration.

But in literary culture, things look bleak. For a century that started out with such wise and valuable critics as Van Wyck Brooks and Edmund Wilson and Suzanne Langer, and saw its middle age in the wonderful company of Alfred Kazin and John W. Aldridge, the prospects for the next century seem less plausible. Great literature demands great critics, and though it may well be that all of us who are writing fiction today truly deserve the company of the myopic – and at the same time megalomaniac – crew of neo-Marxists and feminists and post-postmodern academic cul- ture vultures, to have to live with them is not thrilling, to say the least.

On the one hand they puff up second- and third-rate work because it serves their theses, rather than (as the great critics have always done) dis- cover their values in the great works of the time. On the other, they ignore entire areas of creation because the works do not suit their already- decided-upon values. But more important for the situation of the reader is the fact that none of these critics writes well enough to have much ap- peal for the layperson. This leaves the playing field to the contest be- tween the reviewers and the publicists. And since many of the best reviewers are novelists (among whom the best of these is John Updike) and put their best efforts, as they should, into writing fiction rather than just writing about it, the formation of public taste is usually worked on full-time only by the publicists.

I don't mean to attack publicists. They do what they're supposed to do, which is bring the books to public attention. God help the writer these days who doesn't have a good one working on his or her behalf. But with hundreds of novels published each year and a limited dollar amount in the pockets of potential readers, someone has to try to do more than merely assert that whatever book they're touting at the moment is the best book of the moment. Yet there are fewer and fewer voices speaking with critical authority, style, and intelligence in an effort to help the reading public sort things out.

The results are paradoxical, and for serious readers, not to mention serious writers, somewhat demoralizing. On the one hand, we have limited, what we might call "pocket" successes – American versions of the European art novel that find a devoted audience, novels by, say, Joyce Carol Oates or Jayne Anne Phillips. And then there is the work put forward in certain academic circles because it stands as evidence of a particular presentation of American culture. (I'm using the word culture rather than life because this sort of book, for me, at least, never really lives except as part of a larger argument about society.) The works of Don DeLillo and Paul Auster come to mind here. At the other extreme is the big-seller list, which is by and large pretty awful stuff, with Stephen King and Tom Clancy standing at the top of the pile. Now and then a movie tie-in or some cultural turn will kick a serious book up on the list, a novel by E. L. Doctorow or Edith Wharton or Amy Tan or Toni Morrison. But for the most part, mainstream readers elevate the awful to stardom. It's been that way since the creation of the best-seller list just before World War I and it will certainly not get better for a while, if at all.

For the past few seasons, for example, the novels of Mississippi lawyer John Grisham have been all the rage. When I picked up a copy of *The Firm* – having been surrounded at family occasions by relatives urging me to do it – in hopes of some fast-paced reading pleasure, the kind I used to look for in those sea stories of Forester and in science fiction and for the past few decades have found in a select band of spy novelists and thriller writers from John Le Carré to Thomas Harris, I was terribly disappointed. But not surprised. The same thing happened years before when

I tried out of desperation to fend off the Robert Ludlum crowd. It's all mediocre fare, with no real sense of language or psychology or plot beyond the melodramatic. Danielle Steel and the other romance writers are no better. "He entered her and they made love all night." That sentence of Steel's has stayed with me since I first read it. You can't get much worse and still be writing published fiction. But anything this woman touches turns to money. So that's the good news and bad news about the American reading public, as John Gardner used to say: "The good news is that in actual numbers more people are reading today than ever before in the history of the planet. The bad news is that they're reading mostly shit."

Commercial publishers don't offer all that much optimism. Even as they produce sales figures slightly above last year's, you notice that the dreck makes up most of the sales. Perhaps it's always been so, but lately it seems more so than usual. As the late publisher Sol Stein once put it so ironically and truly, "it's only those books that transmit the culture from one generation to the next" that are being left off the lists these days. And so-called mid-list writers, wonderfully entertaining and serious all in one, find themselves driven out of the marketplace for... where? If the trend keeps moving in this direction, an entire generation of gifted but non-best-selling American fiction writers are headed toward oblivion long before death.

"But look at all the book clubs just here in Washington," a friend of mine pointed out to me the other day when I presented him with this portrait of literary culture and readership in chaos. "There are readers all over the place." And it's true. Washington is a city of reading groups and I'm sure there are many cities like it across the country. And in the schools across the country there's no dearth of bright readers. Those kids lying on cushions in that classroom in Huntsville, Texas, for example. Or the Jane Austen fans at the private girls' school in Troy, New York, where I visited one afternoon to witness a discussion of *Mansfield Park* that was as heated and intense as a squash game. Or the Washington, D.C., public school classes where the PEN/Faulkner Foundation sends visiting fiction writers to discuss their work with interested students.

It's not that we're sliding back into some dark age of total illiteracy. But as we lurch toward the millennium, the news for the future of the American readership is growing exceedingly strange. McLuhanite doomsayers are appearing on all sides. Ivan Illich, for example, argues in his new book *In the Vineyard of the Text* that "the age of the bookish text seems to be passing." The advent of the personal computer and the electronic era, Illich goes on, has irrevocably undermined the primacy of the book and altered our way of pursuing knowledge. Such faddish visions make the writer's heart sink.

But it's the reader in me more than the writer that takes the greatest offense. Having grown up in the time of the Big Talk about the Death of the Novel and now finding myself on the verge of an epoch in which the Big Talk focuses on the Death of Literature and possibly even the Death of the Book itself, all the Jersey rises up in me and wants to spit on the Reeboks of whatever current theologian of culture makes this argument. And there's no help from the academy, either. In exactly that quarter where you think you might find people professing their love of literature and the importance, if not the primacy, of the art of fiction and poetry you meet instead theory-fraught ideologues waving foreign paradigms about in place of Scripture, telling us of every reason under the sun for spending time with a book except the necessary ones.

To know another mind. To know another life. To feel oneself in the heart of another age, in the heart of another human being. To live out the entire trajectory of a human motivation and understand its fullness in time. To move out of ourselves, lifted into another scene, another action, another destiny, so that we might gain a better sense of our own. To warm our spirits by the heat of a fine story, to help us keep the vision (even if illusion) of order in a world constantly on the verge of chaos. Bored theoreticians, losing hold of their own humanity, turn away from these blessings that the novel offers in order to further their own pallid fantasies of the modern spirit. And by shirking their responsibility toward the very humanist tradition that spawned them, they show their contempt not only for their own best (now sadly blighted) tendencies as readers but also for the new generations of potential readers to come, who even now in the elementary schools of urban America are doing their best to prepare themselves – sounding their vowels, making out their letters, clumping them together into stumbling words on the page – to partake of the riches of our culture from Homer to Virginia Woolf to John Edgar Wideman. And for the potential new readers among our immigrant populations. And for the newly educated adults, born here but not born free enough to learn to read as children, new readers such as James the truck driver, my companion at the literacy council Christmas supper.

"TV gets to you after a while," James said to me as we were finishing up our turkey. "And let me tell you, life is tough enough without finding out a way to see it a little better. I learned the hard way, by not learning until now. My mama told us good stories when we were children, but she couldn't write them down. I'm missing a good story like in the old days. So when I get good enough with my reading, that's what I'm going to do."

"Write them down?" I said.

James laughed and chewed a bite of food.

"I don't know if I'd ever get that good. But I would like to read one."

"Talking here with you," I told him, "made me remember the first time I ever heard a story, the first time I ever thought about learning how to read."

"Tell me the story," he said.

I explained that I couldn't because it had been in Russian and all these years I had never found the English version of that tale.

"Well, that's a story by itself," he said. "Remembering it, trying to find it, not finding it. Write that one down. And maybe some time when I get good enough I'll see it on a page."

So this is what I've done.

EDWARD HIRSCH

Following What You Lead: The Mystery of Writing Poetry

[TASTE OF CHICAGO WRITING CONFERENCE]

I want to address, in a somewhat personal way, the process of writing and making poems, a lifelong project that has gotten more rather than less mysterious to me over the years. And I want to use my own experiences with poetry to think about the nature of the creative process itself. I suspect that the specific means and methods of transport are vastly different, but that the underlying processes of the creative mind at work are much the same in all fields. Art is, in some genuine sense, a form of problem solving, a way by which we come to know ourselves, and what the poet does seems to me powerfully akin to the practice of the mathematician, the physicist, the composer, indeed to all those who create what we might call intentional works of the mind. What is it our experiments have in common? Certainly our intellectual and expressive labor, whatever it is, demands patience and craft, obstinacy and determination, disinterestedness and gusto, a long foreground of learning, self-surrender to an idea, absolute concentration. We commit ourselves to discipline and hard work, to long, unstinting, often unrewarding periods of conscious and conscientious work. Yet there is always a point where our voluntary efforts come to an end. Then something else—some unknown force—takes over. In this way we are all explorers setting out for unnamed, unmapped terrain. What is the character of this force? No one knows precisely. For the imagination—as opposed to the strictly rational intellect—is allied to dreams and reveries, to unconscious mechanisms of displacement and identification, of sublimation, projection, condensation. We go to work on our ideas and, hopefully, our ideas go to work in us. We concentrate our days and nights with thought, we sleep and one morning wake up refreshed on another shore.

I myself have been trying to write poetry for more than twenty-five years now, and the mystery of my chosen art form—the splendor and limitation of words, the relationship between passion and form, inspiration and craft, unconscious and conscious elements—has continued to deepen. Writing poetry is a process of disinterested making, a difficult labor, but it is also an abiding pleasure, a summoning and a vocation. I feel very humble, even reverential, before the work and the calling.

Writing poetry didn't start out being very mysterious to me. I just wrote what I felt, or what I thought I felt, which was obscure but pressing. I started writing in high school the way almost everyone begins to write. I wasn't interested in poetry per se—I didn't really even know what poetry was—but I needed to figure out my feelings and put them on paper. I wrote out of emotional desperation and writing became a way of getting through to myself, maybe even of constructing myself. Emotion was and remains at the core of it. I have never forgotten Ezra Pound's precept, which I stumbled upon as a teenager, "Only emotion endures."

Of course in those days—since I wasn't troubled by a prior knowledge of poetry—I loved everything I wrote. I thought it was terrific, even though no one else could make heads or tails of it. It was obscure even to me, perhaps that's why I liked it so much. Over the years I have struggled more and more with my own poetic craft. Writing has gotten harder rather than easier, and I have been more and more dissatisfied with my own work, though of course I know I'm a much better writer today than when I started out. Now I seek clarity in making language answerable to experience, indeed, in making language an experience in and of itself. The problem of slowly and somewhat unwittingly becoming aware of the intricacies involved in one's art form seems to me common to practitioners in all fields. Ever since I first discovered them, I have taken heart from Chardin's words (perhaps retouched by Diderot) in the closing years of the eighteenth century: "He who has not felt the difficulties of his art does nothing that counts; he who . . . has felt them too soon does nothing at all."

What is a poet, specifically, but a linguistic maker, a user of words? "I gotta use words when I talk to you," T. S. Eliot wrote despairingly in the first half of our century, and indeed there's the rub. Words are our vehicle and our commerce, our hopeless means of engagement, our particular way of communicating (and miscommunicating) with each other, of not only articulating but also creating experience. We are what we say. Or perhaps we are not. I began to intuit this in college when I first fell in love with poetry. Falling in love with a way of using language, with literature, with individual works, is, I suspect, as mysterious and unlikely as any other kind of love. One feels that turbulent alertness and intense awakening, that poignant welling up of attention in the presence of the beloved. You feel it and you never want to let it go again. You weren't aware that you were waiting to be called, but when it happens you just get up and follow. Not much had prepared me for the experience. I knew my grandfather had written poems, but he died when I was eight years old and I'd never read anything he'd written: none of his poems survived him. He wrote them in the backs of his books, either in Hebrew or Yiddish, from right to left, and after he died all his books were given away. Sometimes I have imagined that I have tried to recreate his work since he was a poet without poems. No one else I knew wrote poetry, or even read it. I wasn't exactly sure that there even *were* any living poets. Certainly I'd never met any.

Nothing else ever spoke to me with the intensity, the sheer meaningfulness, of poetry. I knew that I had found what I was unknowingly seeking on the day my freshman Humanities teacher—a petite woman with an immense vocabulary, the only person I'd ever met who spoke in completely formed sentences—stood up in class and started talking about Achilles' inconsolable mourning over the death of his friend Patroclus. I felt something obscure opening inside me, some door that never again would be closed. Here is the passage in Richmond Lattimore's translation. It's from Book 18 of *The Iliad*. Nestor's son has just given Achilles the ghastly message that his dearest friend, his brother in arms, had been killed wearing Achilles' own armor; indeed, now they are fighting over his naked body.

> He spoke, and the black cloud of sorrow closed on Achilleus.
> In both hands he caught up the grimy dust, and poured it
> over his head and face, and fouled his handsome countenance,
> and the black ashes were scattered over his immortal tunic.
> And he himself, mightily in his might, in the dust lay
> at length, and took and tore at his hair with his hands,
>   and defiled it.

Years later I discovered this same passage poignantly recreated in Christopher Logue's adaptation of Books 16–19 entitled *War Music*. Logue even more acutely captures Achilles' unbearable agony over the loss of his friend. The passage still gives me chills. I feel it like a blow, as if I have been slapped across the face. It takes the top of my head off, as Emily Dickinson said a poem should do. Here it is:

> Down on your knees, Achilles. Farther down.
> Now forward on your hands and put your face into the dirt,
> And scrub it to and fro.
>   Grief has you by the hair with one
> And with the forceps of its other hand
> Uses your mouth to trowel the dogshit up;
> Watches you lift your arms to Heaven; and then
> Pounces and screws your nose into the filth.
>   Gods have plucked drawstrings from your head,
> And from the template of your upper lip
> Modelled their bows.
>   Not now. Not since
> Your grieving reaches out and pistol-whips
> That envied face, until
> Frightened to bear your black, backbreaking agony alone,
> You sank, throat back, thrown back, your voice
> Thrown out across the sea to reach your Source.

At eighteen I was riveted by Achilles' grief, by the long necessary work of mourning, by the anguished poetry of loss, and was never afterward quite the same. It opened up some grief inside me I didn't realize I had already experienced. I recognized Achilles' feeling and thereafter I clung to poetry the way a drowning man clings to a floating oar . . .

I think of writing poetry as a journey to the interior. It is a distinct process of descent, of going downward and inward, of moving past habitual associations, of surrendering to an idea, deranging the senses. For me there are two root impulses to the writing of lyric poems. The first is to descend into the welter, the muck and mire of your emotional life, and to come out with something lucid and human. The second is to make a work that stands apart from your own feelings about it, something passionate and true. The impulse to leave something behind, something lasting that speaks against our vanishing, may be the deeper and more defining enterprise. I'll never forget sitting in my dormitory room and reading one of Gerard Manley Hopkins's late so-called terrible sonnets. The outside world disappeared for me—the world of my friends, my teachers, my college—and I was alone with a naked human voice.

> I wake and feel the fell of dark, not day.
> What hours, O what black hours we have spent
> This night! what sights you, heart, saw; ways you went!
> And more must, in yet longer light's delay.
>   With witness I speak this. But where I say
> Hours I mean years, mean life. And my lament
> Is cries countless, cries like dead letters sent
> To dearest him that lives alas! away.
>
>   I am gall, I am heartburn. God's most deep decree
> Bitter would have me taste: my taste was me;
> Bones built in me, flesh filled, blood brimmed the curse.
>   Selfyeast of spirit a dull dough sours. I see
> The lost are like this, and their scourge to be
> As I am mine, their sweating selves; but worse.

I read this and feel as if the poet is speaking directly to me, to God, to no one, not only articulating but also dramatizing something I hadn't known I knew, something I had perhaps tried not to know, something lost inside the self. He seems to speak from the heart with tremendous immediacy, and yet the poem is also a sonnet, fourteen highly musical and grieving lines, a perfectly constructed lament. I had found a poet who demonstrated—as the Greeks believed—that there is no conflict between possession and technical accomplishment, inspiration and form.

There is a fundamental difference between keeping diaries, writing essays, and making poems. You keep a diary or a journal in order to record what happens to you, seemingly for your own purposes. You write an essay to make an argument or case, to embody a position, however subtle or complex. There is a reader on the not too distant horizon. You write poems to let the language speak through you, to become its vehicle. W. B. Yeats once said that "rhetoric is a quarrel with others, poetry is a quarrel with oneself." He was in effect echoing John Stuart Mill's notion that "rhetoric is heard, poetry is overheard." This puts the poem in a different relationship to the reader. The lyric poem is the most intimate form of literary discourse. It is the social act of a solitary maker. You feel, in the poems I love best, as if you are in the presence of the heart's voice arguing with itself. "I am certain of nothing but of the holiness of the Heart's affections and the truth of Imagination," Keats writes. The poet addresses no one or God, some version of him or herself, some version of the great dead, but ultimately reaches the living reader. I find the idea of language, of lyric poetry itself, immensely hopeful. That's why no poem is too despairing for me, too dark or nihilistic. Even when John Clare writes, "I am, yet what I am, none cares or knows./My friends forsake me like a memory lost,/I am the self-consumer of my woes," he still situates his feeling in language. Despair is a turning away from human commerce, it is silence.

I don't know if I will ever fully understand the relationship in writing poetry between conscious making and unconscious expression. Every writer has had the experience of being surprised in the act of writing, of putting down something stranger and more interesting than what you had planned. You try to follow that thought, that impulse of words, wherever it leads you. It is a hunch, a cloud that you are trying to turn into a shower. This is related to risk—your willingness to take risks—because where it is taking you is often frightening. Grief may have you by the hair, it may be using your mouth to trowel up something foul. There is a tremendous amount we have internalized that tells us not to say certain things, to avoid certain subjects. The internal censors are always hard at work standing guard. They are ever-vigilant. One of the liberating things about writing poetry is the refusal to be silenced. It is a secret that can no longer be kept secret, a refusal that demands emotional courage. There is a good reason that Orpheus—the one who descends into the underworld to retrieve his beloved, who loses her in the process and takes on the grievous song of mourning—is the archetypal figure of the poet.

One mystery of writing poetry is that you are following something that you must also lead. The intuition has to find a body and a form. The writer is both vehicle and creator, instrument and composer. All poems are experiments in language. So, too, poems beget other poems, like progeny. Inexperienced writers seem to think of writing and reading as entirely separate activities, but in fact they are part and parcel of the same activity, the same project. You get most of your "inspiration," your ideas, your models, by internalizing what you have read. I am always stunned to discover young writers who aren't devouring the work of other writers, who aren't allowing themselves to be influenced. One peculiarity of writing poetry is that the less you read the more you sound like every other amateur Victorian poet who ever wrote, the more you sound like everyone else. The more you read the more you enter the stream of language, the changing discourse of poetry, and the better chance you have of sounding your own note.

I myself went through an extended poetic apprenticeship. For years I tried desperately to sound like John Donne, George Herbert, and Andrew Marvell. I was especially interested in developing poetic conceits, in learning how to construct arguments in poetry. I would have become a seventeenth-century poet if I had been offered the opportunity. But sometime during my mid-twenties I decided to stop imitating the diction of metaphysical poetry and to apply the language of argumentation to my own subject matter and experience. I had gone to Keats and Shelley for primacy of feeling, to Hart Crane and Wallace Stevens for richness of language, to William Carlos Williams and Robert Frost for a democratic subject matter, and slowly I began to evolve something I would call my own, something urban, intellectual, romantic. I suppose that in some sense all my poems are arguments with a God I don't believe in. They are arguments about transcendence. I also realized that it wasn't my task to become John Donne, or Emily Dickinson, or W. H. Auden. It was my task to use what I had learned from them to write only those poems I could write, to say what it felt like to live in America in the second half of our century. Thus nothing was already accomplished for me, everything had to be figured out, to be written and inscribed.

Here is the first poem I wrote that I recognized as my own:

SONG

This is a song for the speechless,
the dumb, the mute and the motley,
the unmourned! This is a song for every
pig that was too thin to be slaughtered
last night, but was slaughtered

anyway, every worm that was hooked
on a hook that it didn't expect,
every chair in New York City that has
no arms or legs, and can't speak English,
every sofa that has ever been torn
apart by the children or the dog
and earmarked for the dump, every sheet
that was lost in the laundry, every
car that has been stripped down and
abandoned, too poor to be towed away,
too weak and humble to protest.
Listen, this song is for you even if
you can't listen to it, or join in;
even if you don't have lungs, even
if you don't know what a song is,
or want to know. This song is for
everyone who is not listening tonight
and refuses to sing. Not singing
is also an act of devotion; those
who have no voices have one tongue.

I believe that every poet believes—some more secretly than others—that he is the vehicle of something, that he is entrusted with something, that he is speaking on behalf of something larger than himself. From the ballad singer, who so often praises the virtues of shared experience, to the most isolated of makers, a Christopher Smart or an Emily Dickinson, the poet repairs language and sings against human forgetfulness, against the crisis of amnesia.

What is the relationship between conscious work, the conscientious labor of making, and unconscious development? Pound said that "technique is the test of a man's sincerity," and unquestionably writing poetry demands technique, a certain amount of skill, a willingness to do arduous work, to acquire learning. It is shameful to fail because of not learning your craft, but it is not shameful to fail. I decided a long time ago that I would rather fail at being a poet than succeed at being something else. Poetry writing demands concentration and attention. Happiness is absorption. Simone Weil said that "absolutely unmixed attention is prayer." Always the work at hand becomes the writer's immediate fate.

Paul Valéry spoke of "une ligne donné"—the given line—and suggested that everything else was labor, a matter of making. Baudelaire talked of "the labor by which a revery becomes a work of art." In his 1846 essay "The Philosophy of Composition" Edgar Allan Poe emphasized the conscious method of trial and error. Here is Poe:

> Most writers—poets in especial—prefer having it understood that they compose by a species of fine frenzy—an ecstatic intuition—and would positively shudder at letting the public take a peep behind the scenes at the elaborate and vacillating crudities of thought—at the true purposes seized only at the last moment—at the innumerable glimpses of idea that arrived not at the maturity of full view—at the fully matured fancies discarded in despair as unmanageable—at the cautious selections and rejections—at the painful erasures and interpolations—in a word, at the wheels and pinions—the tackle for scene-shifting—the step-ladders and patches, which, in ninety-nine cases out of the hundred constitute the literary *histrio.*

Poe is here giving enormous preference—and privilege—to the nature of reason in the creative process.

But there is something else. It may be true that we are only given one line, but that line is nonetheless a gift from the unconscious, a hunch, an intuition and perception. The poet is one who often thinks by feeling. I think of the famous Cartesian Cogito ("I think, therefore I am") and remember Paul Valéry's useful poetic revision, "Sometimes I think, and sometimes I am." Not everything can or should be willed. There is a book called *The Creative Process,* edited by Brewster Ghiselin, that I find helpful in thinking about the problem. It shows many thinkers in different fields—composers, visual artists, scientists—worrying the same set of issues. This book reminds us there are many paths to the creative breakthrough. And yet the combination of conscious and unconscious invention is one of the book's recurring motifs. We are reminded that after a long investigative period Kekule solved the chemical problem of the Benzene molecule, a ring rather than a chain of carbon atoms, when in a daydream he saw a snake swallowing its own tail. We hear George Rouault declaring, "In truth, I have painted by opening my eyes day and night on the perceptible world, and also by closing them from time to time that I might better see the vision blossom and submit itself to orderly arrangement."

There is an especially useful memoir by the great mathematician Henri Poincaré in which he talks about working on a mathematical problem—the Fuchian function—in much the same way that a poet speaks of working on a lyric poem. At one point he describes struggling with the same agonizingly difficult problem every day for fifteen days. He simply can't solve the problem he has set himself. Eventually, he has to put the work aside to go to a conference. But on his way to the conference the answer suddenly comes to him out of the blue as he is stepping onto a bus. He knows it is correct, he simply has to go home and verify the theorem at his leisure, which he eventually does. Poincaré calls the answer a sudden illumination, "a manifest sign of long, unconscious inner work."

For me, the moral of this story is that the unconscious will give you gifts; it will help you solve creative problems (or may) on the condition that you consciously work as hard and as long as you can. Absorbed attention, purity of motive, concentration must take you as far as you can possibly go. You can't wait around for inspiration to strike, you might have a very long wait. Unconscious invention is supplementary to conscious invention; it goes on brooding over the problems and issues that are passionately important to the waking mind. You have to do everything you can to induce the spirit and then, if you're lucky, some unknown force may emerge, something may descend.

Inspiration is in-breathing, in-dwelling, and poetry can never be entirely willed—as Plato knew. It is often connected to passion, to mania, to childlike play, to the unconscious itself. The terror of writing comes from the fact that there is always something involved beyond mere willpower and conscious labor. Writers have developed various mediating rituals— Schiller liked the smell of rotten apples coming out from under the lid of his desk, Hart Crane turned up the phonograph as high as possible and drank too much—to help along the process. There are many ways of calling out, "Help me, O Heavenly Muse." You may locate the Muse outside yourself—you may call her Laura (as Petrarch does) or Beatrice (as Dante does), you may name her Mnemosyne (goddess of memory) or Clio (goddess of history). Or you can place it as a force inside yourself, an unknown terrain. Lorca calls it *duende*, the force that takes over the creator, the act of creating in the presence of death. You can call it the collective unconscious (as Jung does) or creative intuition (as Jacques Maritain does), but you are always trying to invoke something that can't be entirely controlled. The wind must blow through you. This is the necessary touch of madness that Plato made so much of, the freedom that terrified him. He said:

> He who without the Muses' madness in his soul comes knocking at the door of poesy and thinks that art will make him anything fit for to be called a poet, finds that poetry which he indites in his sole senses is beaten hollow by the poetry of madmen.

Poetry is in this view dangerous, it is allied closely to madness, it is not entirely at the dispensation of the poet's conscious will or intellect. "Poetry is not like reasoning, a power to be exerted according to the determination of the will," Shelley writes in his romantic defense of poetry. "A man cannot say, 'I will compose poetry.' The greatest poet even cannot say it; for the mind in creation is as a fading coal which some invisible influence, like an inconstant wind, awakens to transitory brightness."

Who has not longed for sudden illuminations, epiphanic moments of pure being? What poet has not longed to believe with Shelley, that great apostle of the imagination, that "poetry redeems from decay the visitations of the divinity in man." Maybe that's why so much lyric poetry has the quality and character of prayer. It takes faith to write. Or a longing for faith. Or an invocation of faith. Much about writing can be learned from others—and everything that can be learned should be learned—but ultimately you come up against yourself, against what used to be called "the soul."

There is a poem by W. S. Merwin, called simply "Berryman," that gets at what I'm talking about. In this poem Merwin remembers the advice of the "older" poet (John Berryman was in his thirties then) to the young aspirant in the years after the Second World War. As Merwin recalls, Berryman warned him not to lose his arrogance too soon or to replace it with vanity; he advised him to paper his wall with rejection slips, he suggested that he get down on his knees in the corner and literally pray to the Muse. He remembers how Berryman trembled with the vehemence of his feelings about poetry, and how he argued that the great transfiguring presence in poetry is always passion. (He also praised invention and movement.) The young poet had scarcely started to read. He asks how you can ever be certain that what you write is actually any good at all and the older poet—wisely, poignantly, agonizingly—tells him that you can never be truly sure about your writing, that you have to live (and die) with the uncertainty, and that if you have to be absolutely sure then you shouldn't write. I find this advice moving, passionate, and true. The process of writing poems—indeed the process of creating almost anything of value—is painful, messy, joyous. It is a spiritual exercise, a continual and laborious experience of trying to get something right. It is a great adventure, a splendid and mysterious way of being in the world, and I welcome you to it. The writer is always self-elected. So elect yourself. Read everything you can, work hard at knowing your craft, accept the doubt and the agony, trust your own experience, your own intuition, get down on your knees and pray, "Help me, O Heavenly Muse . . ."

GARY PAUL NABHAN

The Far Outside

[ART OF THE WILD CONFERENCE]

> Any good poet, in our age at least, must begin with the
> scientific view of the world; and any scientist worth listening
> to must be something of a poet, must possess the ability to
> communicate to the rest of us his sense of love and wonder at
> what his work discovers.
>
> – Edward Abbey, *The Journey Home*

I was in a small room in Alaska when I heard it. That was part of the
trouble. I was supposed to be keeping my attention on what was being
said in the room; after all, this was a nature writing symposium. But from
where I sat I could hear ravens coming in to roost in the spruce trees
above us, and was wondering how their calls were different from those of
the Chihuahuan ravens down in the Sonoran desert, where I live. I could
look out the windows and see bald eagles swooping over the waters of the
sound. Worse yet, I already had the stain and smell of salmonberries on
my hands, and had been perplexed all morning as to why the ripe berries
on two adjacent bushes were entirely different colors.

It was then that I heard it. A familiar warble came out of the well-
educated, widely read humanist/poet a few chairs away from me. She asserted a truism that I had heard in one form or another for nearly thirty
years:

"Each of us has to go *inside* before we can go *outside!* How can we give
any meaning to the natural world until each individual finds out who he or
she is as a human being, until each of us finds our own internal source of
peace?"

Queasy. I immediately felt nauseated. Indisposed. Something she had said had stuck in my craw. Instantly, I was so out of sorts that I had to leave the room. Our moderator followed me out to the porch, where I gasped for air.

"Are you *okay?*" she asked earnestly. "You looked *green* all of a sudden."

"I dunno." I breathed deeply, and looked up at the crisp blue sky. "I must be . . . uh . . . under the weather a little. Let me see if some fresh air will help . . . If you don't mind, I had better go for a walk."

As I ambled along, I wondered about what had set me off. I wandered around on a rainforest trail, trying to spiral in on what in that room had disoriented me.

First, I felt uncomfortable with the notion that we can give the natural world "its meaning." The plants and animals that I have observed most diligently over twenty years as a field biologist hardly seem to be waiting for me to give *them* meaning. Instead, most humans want to feel as though *we* are meaningful, and so we project *our* meanings upon the rest of the world. We read meaning into other species' behavior, but with few exceptions, they are unlikely to do the same toward us.

Humans may, in fact, be rare even among primates in the attention we give to a wide range of other species' tracks, calls, and movements. To paraphrase one prominent primatologist, "If their inattention to their neighbors other than predators is any indication, most monkeys are extremely poor naturalists." The same can be said of many other wild animals that live in sight of, and in spite of, human habitations.

While it may somehow be good for *us* to think and write about plants and animals, I am reminded of John Daniel's humbling insight while hopping through a snake-laden boulder field: the snakes were not fazed by his thoughts, fears, or needs. As Daniel has written in *The Trail Home* (1992):

> The rattlesnakes beneath the boulders instructed me, in a way no book could have, that the natural world did not exist entirely for my comfort and pleasure; indeed, that it did not particularly care whether my small human life continued to exist at all.

I walked along, and my restlessness increased as I considered the premise put forth in that room: The shortest road to wisdom and peace with the world is that which turns inward. I will not argue that meditation, psychotherapy, and philosophical reflection are unproductive, but I simply can't accept that *inward* is the only, or the best way, for everyone to turn. The more disciplined practitioners of contemplative traditions can turn inward and still get beyond the self, but many others simply stumble into self-indulgence.

As Robinson Jeffers suggested more than half a century ago, it may be just as valid to turn outward.

> The whole human race spends too much emotion on itself. The happiest and freest man is the scientist investigating nature or the artist admiring it, the person who is interested in things that are not human. Or if he is interested in human beings, let him regard them objectively as a small part of the great music.

Finishing my walk among the great music of crashing waves and hermit thrushes, I conceded that the wisest, most inspired people I knew had all taken this second path, heading for what I call the Far Outside. It is the path found when one falls into "the naturalist's trance," the hunter's pursuit of wild game, the *curandera*'s search for hidden roots, the fisherman's casting of the net into the current, the water-witch's trust of the forked willow branch, and the rock climber's fixture on the slightest surfaces of a cliff face. Oddly, it is hanging onto that cliff beyond the reach of the safety net of civilization where one may gain the deepest sense of what it is to be alive. As Arctic writer and ethnographer Hugh Brody says of his predilection for working in the most remote human communities and wildest places he can find, "it is at the periphery that I can come to understand the center."

Unlike conditions within the metropolitan grid where it seems that we have got nature surrounded, the Far Outside still offers the comic juxtapositions, the ones worthy of a Gary Larsen cartoon. The flood suddenly looms large, before Noah can get his family onto the ark full of animals; the bugs in the test tube have the last say about the entire experiment.

When I returned home to the Stinkin' Hot Desert, I had an urge to see how an elder from another culture might view this apparent dichotomy between inward and outward paths, or, for that matter, the dichotomy between culture and nature. I drove a hundred miles across the desert to see a seventy-four-year-old O'odham farmer who had worked all his life "outdoors": tending native crops, chopping wood, driving teams of horses, gathering cactus fruit, hunting, and building ceremonial houses for his tribe's rain-bringing rites. He was consistently wise in ways that my brief bouts with Jungian analysis, *zazen* practice, and Franciscan prayer had not enabled me to be. And I knew that because he had had a brush with death over the last year, he had been made sedentary and forced to be alone, housebound, for a longer time than ever before in his entire life. He sat on an old wooden bench, a crutch on either side of him, looking out at a small field that he would not be able to plant this year. I asked him what he had been working over in his mind during the last few months.

"I'd like to make a trip," he said nonchalantly for a man who had only once traveled beyond the limits of the desert – all the way to Gallup – and who now lived at the end of his life less than thirty miles from where he was born.

"Before I die, I'd like to go over there to the ocean," he nodded to the southwest, where the Sea of Cortez lay a hundred miles away. It was a sacred place for the desert O'odham, where they used to go as pilgrims for salt, and for songs. My elderly friend paused, then continued.

"Yes, I would like to hear the birds there in the sea. I would like to hear those ocean birds sing in my native language."

"In O'odham ha-neoki?" I asked, and I must have looked surprised that he felt the birds spoke in *his* language, for he then offered to explain his comment, as if it had been scribbled in a shorthand indiscernible to me.

"Whenever my people used to walk over there to the ocean for salt, they would stand on the edge and listen to those birds sing. And they are in many of the songs we still sing today, even though we haven't walked or ridden horses there since the hoof-and-mouth quarantines in the forties. In the old days, they didn't start to sing those songs while they were still at the ocean. No, the people would go back home, and then, some night, those ocean birds would begin singing in their dreams. That's where our songs come from. They would come to our medicine men, from the ocean, in their dreams. Maybe the ones who play the violin would hear them in their sleep, and their voices would turn up in their fiddle tunes. Maybe the *pascola* dancers would hear the way they flew, and it would end up in the way they sounded when they danced with their rattles. Those birds have ended up in our songs, and I want to hear them at the ocean before I die."

What struck me about my friend's last request was his desire to hear those birds for himself at the edge of the ocean. For a lifelong dweller in a riverless desert, the ocean must be a landscape wilder than the imagination, truly unfathomable. In the end, he sought to juxtapose his culture's aural imagery of ocean birds with what the birds themselves were saying. He desired to directly experience nature, as a measure of the cultural symbols and sounds he had carried with him most of his life.

My friend's songs and stories are conversant with and responsive to what we often refer to as "outer reality." This larger landscape is not superfluous or irrelevant to his culture's literature, music, or ways of healing. When I arrived at his home once years ago, I saw him carrying into the kitchen a mockingbird that he had captured in a seed trap, killed, and carefully butchered, in order to cook the meat up and feed it to his grandson. Mockingbirds are not simply good mimics, they are irrepressibly loquacious; his grandson was not. In fact, the boy was nearly three years old and had not spoken a word. Concerned, my friend recalled the sympathetic ritual of his people for curing such difficulties: feed the mute on the songbird's flesh. He will have the best chance of being able to express himself if he ingests the wild world around him. In the O'odham language, the words for curing, wildness, and health come from the same root.

This is where inner and outer become not a duality, but a dynamic, like every breath we take. We are *inspired* by what surrounds us; we take it into our bodies, and after some rumination, we respond with *expression*. What we have inside us, is, ultimately, always of the larger, wilder world. Nature, then, is not just "out there," beyond the individual. That O'odham boy now has seed, bird, and O'odham history in his very muscles, in the cells of his tongue, in his reverberating voice box.

Lynn Margulis has recently pointed out that thousands of other such lives are literally inside each so-called human "individual." For every cell of our own genetic background that we embody, there are a thousand times more cells of other species within and on each of our bodies. It would be more fitting to imagine each human corpus as a diverse wildlife habitat than to persist with the illusion of the individual self. Or better, each of us is really a corpus of *stories:* bacteria duking it out for the final word in our mouths; fungi having clandestine affairs between our toes; other microbes collaborating on digesting the world within our intestines; archetypal images from our evolutionary past roaming through our nerve synapses, testing our groin muscles against our brain tissue.

If I could distill into a single sentence what I have learned during a thousand and one nights working as a field biologist, waiting around campfires while mist-netting bats, running lines of live traps, or pressing plants, it would be this: Each plant or animal has a story of some unique way of living in this world. By tracking their stories down to the finest detail, our own lives can somehow be informed, and perhaps, enriched. The zoologist who radio-collars a mountain lion may call his research a range utilization analysis, but he is simply tracking that critter's odyssey. A botanist may refer to the adaptive strategy of a cactus, but she surmises that by carefully recording, by chapter and verse, how the plant endures and prevails, despite droughts, freezes, or heat waves. An ecologist interested in nutcrackers' dispersal of pine seeds is slowly learning the language of the forest, and the birds are his newly found verbs.

Perhaps due to what Paul Ehrlich calls "physics envy," many biologists feel inclined to mask their recording of stories in shrouds of numbers, jargon, and theory. We find their remarkable insights buried beneath technobabble about life histories, optimal foraging tests, or paleoecological reconstructions. However, most of them are merely tracing the trajectory of another life as it demonstrates ways to survive in the Far Outside. In *Writing Natural History* (1988), two-time Pulitzer Prize winner E. O. Wilson tells of the struggle scientists have simply to be storytellers.

> Scientists live and die by their ability to depart from the tribe and go out into an unknown terrain and bring back, like a carcass neatly speared, some new discovery or new fact or theoretical insight and lay it in front of the tribe; and then they all gather and dance around it. Symposia are held in the National Academy of Sciences and prizes are given. There is fundamentally no difference from a paleolithic campsite celebration . . .

In short, scientists, too, grapple with the challenge of telling the unheard-of stories that may move their tribes. And yet it is tragic to realize how few of these stories any of us will ever glimpse. In *The Diversity of*

Life (1992), it is E. O. Wilson again who reminds us that we have only the crudest of character sketches, let alone any understanding of the plots involved, for most of these floral and faunal narratives.

> Even though some 1.4 million species of organisms have been discovered (in the minimal sense of having specimens collected and formal scientific names attached), the total number alive on the earth is somewhere between 10 and 100 million . . . Of the species given scientific names, fewer than 10 percent have been studied at a level deeper than gross anatomy. [Intensively studied species make up] . . . a still smaller fraction, including colon bacteria, corn, fruit flies, Norway rats, rhesus monkeys, and human beings, altogether comprising no more than a hundred species.

Try to imagine the still untold stories, the sudden flowerings, the cataclysmic extinctions, the episodic turnovers in dominance, the failed attempts at mutualistic relationships, and the climaxes that took hundreds of years to achieve. In every biotic community there are story lines that fiction writers would give their eyeteeth for: Desert tortoises with allegiances to place lasting upwards of forty thousand years, dwarfing any dynasty in Yoknapatawpha County. Fidelities between hummingbird and montane penstemon that make the fidelities in Port William, Kentucky, seem like puppy love. Dormancies of lotus seeds that outdistance Rip Van Winkle's longest nap. Promiscuities between neighboring oak trees that would make even Nabokov and his Lolita blush. Or all-female lizard species with reproductive habits more radical than anything in lesbian literature.

And yet, with the myriad stories around and within us, how many of them do we recognize as touching our lives in any way? Most natural history essays are so limited in their range of plot, character development, and emotive currents that Joyce Carol Oates has come to an erroneous, near-fatal assumption about nature itself. In her essay "Against Nature," Oates claims that nature "inspires a painfully limited set of responses in 'nature writers' . . . REVERENCE, AWE, PIETY, MYSTICAL ONENESS."

If we look at what most environmental journalists offer, we see an even more limited set of "news" stories: 1) that someone momentarily succeeded in disrupting the plans of the bastards who are ruining the world; and 2) that the bastards are still ruining the world. Structurally, most newspaper and magazine journalists who ostensibly cover biological diversity tell the same gloom-and-doom story over and over, with virtually nothing substantial about the nonhuman lives embedded in that diversity. One week *Paradise Lost* is told with the yew tree as the victim in the temperate rain forest; the next, the scene has shifted to Indonesia for the Bali mynah, but the plot is still the same.

I believe that human existence is being degraded by our ignorance of these diverse stories. In stark contrast to the O'odham elder's dreams, fewer and fewer creatures are inhabiting the dreams of those in mainstream society. I know another elderly man who lives in the midst of metropolitan Phoenix. Although he is a few years younger than my friend the Indian farmer, he seems far closer to death; I can feel it every time I visit him. He, too, was formerly an outdoorsman and farmer, skilled with horses, hunting, building, and wood carving. But now he has emphysema and can't even go outside and sit, as the contaminated air of Phoenix is so vile. Yet that is not all that is killing him. Confined to a hermetically sealed tract house, he sits in front of a television all day long and hears just three stories repeated *ad nauseam:* 1) Saddam Hussein and other foreign despots are out to get us; 2) substance-abusing street gangs are out to get us; and 3) mutant microbes are out to get us. He seems drained of all resilience, a man without hope. He has lost all contact with the wildlife, the Far Outside that had been his source of renewal most of his life.

Harking back to William Carlos Williams, we might say that society pays little attention to these myriad lives, but people die for lack of contact with them every day. As with our teeth, what we don't pay attention to is likely to disappear. By the end of this decade, 25,000 species — 25,000 distinctive ways of living in this world — are likely to be lost unless we begin to learn of these beings in ways that move us sufficiently to curtail our destructive habits.

And that is where scientists cannot do the work by themselves. As E. O. Wilson admits, the capacity to tell of these vanishing lives in compelling ways is dreadfully constrained by the stylistic conventions of technical scientific journals. In *Writing Natural History*, he argues that

the factual information that we get and the new metaphors created out of science somehow have to be translated into the language of the storyteller — by film, by speech, by literature, by any means that will make it meaningful and powerful for the human mind. . . . And the storyteller has always had this central role in societies: of translating that information in forms that played upon the great mythic themes and used the rhythms and the openings . . . the body . . . and the closures that make up literature.

Now, more urgently than ever before, we all need to come face to face with other lives in the Far Outside, not just the Bali mynah and the Pacific yew, but the fungi between our toes as well. Imagine what might happen if some of those who now turn inward, apprenticing themselves to all kinds of gurus, priests, therapists, and masters, would turn outward, as apprentices to other species: Komodo dragons, marbled murrelets, desert pupfish, beer-making yeasts, Texas wild rice, or Okeechobee gourds.

I can't help but wonder if the dilemma of our society is not unlike that of the mute child who needs to eat the songbird in order to speak. Unless we come to embody the songs from the Far Outside, we will be left dumb before an increasingly frightening world. But that is just the first step. Once we have begun to express in our own ways the stories inspired by those other lives, we may need to keep seeking them out, to constantly compare the images we have conjured up with the beings themselves.

It is time to leave this room, and go Outside, farther than we have ever gone together before. It is time to hear the seabirds singing at the edge of the world, and bring them back, freshly, into our dreams.

PATTIANN ROGERS

Twentieth-Century Cosmology and the Soul's Habitation

[SITKA SYMPOSIUM FOR HUMAN VALUES]

I'm very curious about the grid upon which we mentally place ourselves in time and space. There must be a grid of some kind there for each of us, a visual scaffolding, for balance, for orientation. Where and how do we envision ourselves located in time and space? Born in a certain year? At a certain location? By calendar? By map?

But is there more than that in our vision? Do we establish shapes and patterns that form boundaries of history and place inside of which we see ourselves and by which we define ourselves? Do we have an underlying conception of our spatial location in the world when we are out walking, or traveling by air, or inside our homes, here and now? What exactly is the "here and now" for our culture? And does this placing of ourselves in the universe affect our structure of moral values, the way we order our experiences, the way we explain our origins to ourselves?

They must be related. What does it mean to our image of family, landscape, art, to believe that light travels at a constant speed, that light falling through the forest at this moment left the surface of the sun nine minutes before, or that when we look up into the stars we are seeing back through billions of years? What a strange conception – that light carries not only knowledge but time and distance as well.

What exactly is our cosmology, then, the cosmology of our culture today, and how much does it affect our thinking? Does our cosmology permeate the language in subtle ways, the language then structuring our perceptions? These are questions of interest to me, and I don't have all the answers to them.

I'm going to define cosmology as the story of the universe, the explanation of the origin and history and processes of the universe, an explanation that creates the structure upon which we locate ourselves and define ourselves in relation to the objects we observe around us, and by which we also address our own origins and our nature.

Edward R. Harrison, in *Cosmology, the Science of the Universe,* states the importance of cosmology in this way:

> Every society creates universes; not only do these universes reflect the societies, but each universe controls the history and destiny of its society. The most powerful and influential ideas in any society are those that relate to the universe; they shape history, inspire civilizations, foment wars, create empires and establish political systems.

Previous cultures have invented a variety of cosmologies. Some have told stories of magic, stories that explained everything by the motives and actions of ambient spirits inhabiting the natural world and fashioned in the image of humankind. The cosmology of mythology constructed a universe in which the spirits of magic retreated and became remote gods. Anthropocentric cosmologies pictured human beings at the center of the universe, above the beasts, occupying a place of importance, next to the angels, possessing the attention of the creator of all things. During the Middle Ages cosmology and religion were one.

But according to Harrison, "no persons living in the twentieth century can claim to be educated if they are unaware of the *modern* vision of the physical universe and the history of the magnificent concepts that it embodies."

I do believe that the cosmology of our times is at the root of much of what we write and the attitudes and values we espouse, whether we are completely aware of it or not. The world picture we hold today has for the most part been given to us by science, and all of us believe it, to some degree, and even more important, whether we declare we believe in it or not, we act on it, base decisions on it, live by it, and demonstrate daily our faith in it.

I want to state very briefly and simply the way I believe many of us visualize the universe and our place in it, the way I, as a layperson, understand our cosmology. Most of us are so accustomed to these ideas that they may seem ordinary and unsurprising, which proves my contention that this is the cosmology of our time, held closely by the members of our community.

We see ourselves as very tiny beings made up physically of groupings of other even tinier entities, atoms, molecules, cells, and organs. We are made from the dust of old stars. Most of us believe we have risen through natural selection and mutation of genes over many, many millions of years, our bodies being related to all other living bodies on Earth. Beautiful and fine, lovely story, invigorating and incorporating theory, in my opinion.

And we see ourselves as very tiny beings relative to the size of Earth, our planet, third from the Sun in a family of nine planets all circling the Sun, the star closest to us. We understand our Earth is tiny compared to the size of our star. (I remember being taught as a child that the size of Earth compared to the size of the Sun was as a pea relative to a basketball.) The Sun is 740 times more massive than the nine major planets together.

The Sun is tiny compared to the size of the solar system, the solar system to the size of the Milky Way galaxy, the Milky Way to the size of the Andromeda galaxy, which is twice as big, containing 400 billion stars. And yet the Andromeda galaxy is tiny compared to the universe, which contains billions of other galaxies. All of that, up there, going on at this moment.

This, very sketchily, is the way I perceive the structure of our location within the universe, where we place ourselves in the organization of the celestial objects we recognize around us. On the surface of the earth, we visualize and state our location conventionally by imaginary coordinates, latitude and longitude, by North Pole and South Pole, by hemisphere, by relation to the ocean upon which we sail or beside which we live or the mountain range to the east or to the west, by the geographical and political boundaries of our community. If we say "Montana," most of us can visualize the shape and place of that entity on the globe (North Pole at the top), the same with Puget Sound or the Mississippi River or the Panama Canal.

We visualize the shape of Earth and its continents by the maps and photographs we've been shown, some taken from space, geographical maps, geological maps, computer-generated three-dimensional maps, heat-generated maps recorded by satellite. If you imagine at this moment where you are on the globe in Sitka, something visual must occur. This picture comes to us through science and technology.

We believe, so our story goes, that we are being carried on this spinning Earth that turns on its own axis at a speed so fast we can't even feel it. Our Earth, bearing with it one orbiting moon, meanwhile circles and tilts around the Sun, which is itself borne along with the solar system on its path around the center of the Milky Way, the Milky Way and its billions of sun/stars moving as one body – where? Simply away from all other cosmic bodies, a result of the Big Bang theory of the origin of the universe as we currently understand it. We aren't really sitting still at all, but are caught up in this mayhem of motion.

We perceive the time span of our existence, even as a species, as fleeting compared to the life span of some now extinct species (dinosaurs, for example), and we have figures to prove this aspect of our insignificance. Our lives are fleeting compared to the age of the earth, the history of the Sun, the solar system, the Milky Way, a pulsar, a quasar. . . .

The story our cosmology tells is that we exist in a universe of flux, not only the rushing river that can never be stepped in twice, but also stars in the process of being born and dying, our own sun in decline, expending itself. (Could anyone come across an article entitled "The Death of the Sun," as I did recently, and not feel a sudden fear and stillness in the heart?) The mountains that once seemed so sure and enduring to other generations in their cosmologies, we know now that they, too, have risen and will wear away. Floors of the ocean and platforms under the continents shift and slowly collide, greatly altering the surface of the earth. Forests grow up and fall away. Oceans enlarge and decline. Ice sheets form, descend, and retreat. Volcanoes, like Krakatoa, erupt, alter the climate, and affect life on Earth for centuries. Strong, successful species gain ascendancy on the earth, eventually wane and vanish. Civilizations full of vibrant and brilliant minds come and go. Our own bodies, the cells of our brains, finely balanced, die and replace themselves constantly.

We also understand our physical being as the result of very slow, apparently random changes, mutations occurring within the DNA, the hereditary code, gradual transformations and adaptations that took place over a very long period of time. We can witness adaptive evolutionary changes in some animals (insects, small fish, some birds and amphibians) during our own lifetimes. We have watched our own civilization change and alter the earth, eradicate certain diseases, create bacterias, manipulate the development of domesticated animals, affect the environment.

Flux and change are constant, so the story goes.

If human consciousness should play a role in the well-being of the universe, we aren't certain what that role is. Our cosmology seems not to address this issue directly. If there is a power or a creator interested in us (though I think the doubt many of us feel in this regard is so deep and pervasive that the issue is hardly mentioned anymore, at least not in the same breath as our cosmology), we aren't certain in what way that power might manifest itself or what vocabulary is suitable for addressing its existence.

As a result of this cosmology, all of us, I would venture to say, have seen ourselves at some moment or other as "mankind cast aimlessly adrift in a meaningless universe."

To further complicate the story, we have experienced in this century a sudden and continual influx into our culture of massive amounts of information, information that affects the story our cosmology tells, new information published constantly concerning the heavens and the evolutionary processes of stars, the discovery of new elementary particles, information redefining time, detailed and profuse information on the processes by which animal and plant species function and survive, information about the geological history of the earth and extinct species, information about other human cultures past and present, about the human body, the human brain, the human psyche, information about new technologies that radically alter forms of communication, vigorous exploration of both the very large and the microscopic, even invisible neutrinos, books and books on just the history of the violin, for instance, the history of bread, the history of locks and keys – the history of paperweights, for heaven's sake. You name it and at least one person has written a book about it, with many more, we are certain, to come.

I chose at random one page from the *Oxford-Duden Pictorial English Dictionary*, a dictionary that lists some 28,000 objects from a whole range of technical activities and everyday situations. Listed on this one page are 103 terms dealing simply with roofs and roofing.

I don't believe any previous culture has ever had such a massive vocabulary available to it as does ours today. Every word, *every* word, I believe, a possible metaphor.

All of these oceans of information can be daunting enough, but add to that the fact that much of this information is changing and refining itself continually – and the result is often despair. One is almost fearful to utter a declarative sentence unless its implications are so narrow and qualified – say, for example, "This is how I myself personally think I myself alone might possibly have felt just a moment ago maybe" – that it becomes inane.

So, like the universe, we conceive of our cosmology as constantly changing, altering itself, too, according to new data, more refined methods of gathering information. We are reluctant, then, to put our wholehearted faith in all the details of this story, the cosmology as it is constructed today.

This is a very strange and unique facet of our cosmology, that it instructs us not to allow ourselves to fully believe it as it is told today. We must always reserve the right to critically review the cosmology. The cosmology itself tells us this. This is one of its own characteristics, part of its very own tenets and story – its request for suspension of full commitment, its own insistence on a critical eye and mind at work on itself.

This is very different from the cosmologies of past cultures. Our cosmology tells us we must be willing to accept new, corroborated information that may dismiss or alter parts of its story as previously related. The story adjusts and expands. Rigidity is definitely not a part of our cosmology. Science is not rigid. Dogmas are rigid.

So maybe we like this cosmology, the excitement and astonishment of its grand ideas, the vastness and power and mystery of the universe it describes, the beauty of its intricacies, the freedom of thought it affords. Maybe we love the very fact of its openness, its willingness to adapt itself, its willingness to actually respond to us. That is pretty fine and wonderful, I think.

Or maybe we don't like this cosmology. We might be willing and eager to subscribe to seeing a universe in a grain of sand, but a *changing* universe in *every* grain of sand? At every moment? Our cosmology seems at times to describe a universe that takes no cognizance of us, to describe a universe indifferent to us, "a world of quantity, of reified geometry, a world in

which, though there is a place for everything, there is no place for man."
Maybe this is the source of much of the literature of despair, or a literature seeking consolation, the literature of seeking consolation in the natural world on Earth. Maybe.

And if we had been given a choice, perhaps we would have created a
different cosmology. I'm not arguing that this cosmology is right or
wrong, complete or incomplete, eternal or ephemeral, satisfying or disturbing. But I am saying this cosmology is the one that is ours. Not only
does it provide much of the vocabulary and many of the images of our
time, but the way we live and survive physically depends on it. It is integral to our daily lives.

Simply walking out into a wilderness and leaving behind temporarily
the life and the accoutrements of our human communities doesn't mean
we leave behind this cosmology. It's part of our being. We carry it with us
right out onto the tundra, into the rain forest, diving beneath the ocean.
In fact, we understand these very designations — *tundra, rain forest, ocean*
— in part by the light of our cosmology.

The effect of the vision created by our cosmology is evident in Dick
Nelson's description of the experience of surfing in Alaska, in his book
The Island Within.

> Shortly, an even larger series of swells approaches, but I'm far enough out to
> catch the biggest one and prudent enough to make it my last. As I wade ashore, I
> watch the energy of the wave die, rushing to the top of the beach and slipping back
> down again. And I remember its power rising to a crescendo around and under me
> during the final moments of its life, after traversing a thousand miles of ocean from
> its birthplace in a far Pacific storm. The motion that so exalted me was given freely
> by the wave, as the wave was given motion by the wind, as the wind was given mo-
> tion by the storm, as the storm was given motion by the whirl of the atmosphere
> and the turning of the earth itself. Then I remember the sea lions, cradled by the
> same ocean and pleasured by the same waves. All of us here, partaking of a single
> motion. Together and alive.

And again Barry Lopez, in *Offshore: A Journey to the Weddell Sea*, elo-
quently describes this vision onboard the *Nathaniel B. Palmer*, an ice-
breaking scientific research vessel, as it heads for the southern seas:

The bridge, its wings cantilevered over ship and ocean on either side and its vast ability to communicate and to navigate so implicit in its mute antennas, nearly fills one's field of vision. Above it and beyond tonight is the blackest blue sky riven cleanly by the familiar tingling spine of suns, the Galaxy seen edge-on. Watching the bridge move under the stars, feeling the ship's engines thrum in my legs, and standing in a breeze high above the ocean's smooth, dark plain – and then sensing the plunging depth, the shadowed plain of the Peru Basin below, the complex signal codes of the bioluminescence winking there above the basin floor like stars – I thought, this must be sailing.

This vision of place and relationships, this cosmology, is our myth. We carry it with us in our memories, in our gestures, our bones, just as we carry *Hamlet* or the music of Bach or the Christmas story or the vision of our bedroom at home or the act of turning a page in a book or the face of our mother. There's no getting rid of it. No hope of that.

So what do the underlying concepts of this cosmology that we carry with us do to language? We know our language has been greatly enhanced and enlarged through the vocabulary given us by the sciences. We know that much. How do the images presented us through this cosmology, the vision of planets moving in their orbits through space, the solar system intersected by comets and asteroids, for example, affect the frameworks and metaphors upon which we construct our literature? How does the cosmology affect our choices of subject matter, the tone, confident or abject, in the first line of the poem or essay, our stance toward the hour of the day, the way we regard a rookery of sea lions, eagles clasping claws in midair, the arrow-straight morning sun through the window, across the sheets?

I've already suggested that this cosmology may be the source of much of today's literature of despair, or literature that turns inward, becomes solipsistic, literature seeking consolation in some kind of certainty that is perceived as being absent from our cosmology. But are there effects much more subtle?

And even more crucial, how does our cosmology influence our definitions of loyalty, honesty, dignity, art, love?

We can be sure the effects are there, and in order to develop the strongest beliefs possible – beliefs that enable us to act with conviction, dignity, and generosity—we must understand, recognize, and acknowledge the story of our cosmology, which is shaping the attitudes we take toward ourselves and our world, and also our conceptions of our potentialities. We must learn how to grasp our cosmology fully and to infuse it with a sustaining spirituality.

A statement by Bertrand Russell in *A Free Man's Worship* succinctly defines the despair that can rise from our cosmology:

> That man is the product of causes which had no prevision of the end they were achieving; that his origin, his growth, his hopes and fears, his loves and his beliefs, are but the outcome of accidental collocations of atoms; that no fire, no heroism, no intensity of thought or feeling, can preserve a life beyond the grave; that all the labors of the ages, all the devotion, all the inspirations, all the noonday brightness of human genius, are destined to extinction in the vast death of the solar system; and the whole temple of Man's achievement must inevitably be buried beneath the debris of a universe in ruins—all these things, if not quite beyond dispute, are yet so nearly certain, that no philosophy which rejects them can hope to stand. Only within the scaffolding of these truths, only on the firm foundation of unyielding despair, can the soul's habitation be safely built.

The point of departure must be "unyielding despair." We start from the recognition of that point to build the soul's habitation.

Beginning there we should understand that science is in the business of measuring things. Science constructs a model of the universe only from those things that it is able to measure. The model of the universe, the cosmology that science creates, is based on what science is able to measure. It is the fallacy of misplaced concreteness, then, to proclaim that this model is the total reality. The model is not untrue, but only partial, not all-inclusive. If this model were complete, and scientists believed it to be complete, the business of science would come to an abrupt halt. Total truth has not yet been discovered.

Jacob Bronowski in his book *The Origin of Knowledge and Imagination* describes another limitation of any investigation of the universe:

> I believe that the world is totally connected: this is to say, that there are no events anywhere in the universe which are not tied to every other event in the universe. I regard this to some extent as a metaphysical statement, although you will

see, as I develop it in the next lecture, it has a much more down-to-earth content
than that. But I will repeat it: I believe that every event in the world is connected
to every other event. But you cannot carry on science on the supposition that you
are going to be able to connect every event with every other event. . . . It is, therefore, an essential part of the methodology of science to divide the world for any experiment into what we regard as relevant and what we regard, for purposes of that
experiment, as irrelevant.

   We make a cut. We put the experiment, if you like, into a box. Now the moment we do that, we do violence to the connections in the world. We may have the
best cause in the world. I may say, "Well, come on, I am not really going to think
that the light from Sirius is going to affect the reading of this micrometer!" And I
say this although I can see Sirius clear with the naked eye, and I have the impertinence to say that though the light of Sirius affects my rods and cones it is not going
to affect the experiment. Therefore we have always, if I may use another Talmu-
dic phrase, to put a fence round the law, to put a fence round the law of nature that
we are trying to tease out. And we have to say, "For purposes of this experiment
everything outside here is regarded as irrelevant, and everything inside here is regarded as relevant."

Any effort to investigate the universe, whether through science or literature, involves making a cut in the universe, interrupting its wholeness
and unity, and therefore disrupting and ignoring the interconnectedness
of all things. Any investigation, poem, or laboratory experiment involves
saying "certain things are relevant to this investigation and certain things
are not," and once this necessary cut has been made, we have eliminated
any possibility of seeing nature and the universe as a whole, in its entirety.

And from Bronowski later in the same book:

   The act of imagination is the opening of the system so that it shows new connections. I originally put this idea in *Science and Human Values* when I said that every act of imagination is the discovery of likenesses between two things which
were thought unlike. And the example that I gave was Newton's thinking of the
likeness between the thrown apple and the moon sailing majestically in the sky. A
most improbable likeness, but one which turned out to be (if you will forgive the
phrase) enormously fruitful. All acts of imagination are of that kind. They take the
closed system, they inspect it, they manipulate it, and then they find something
which had not been put into the system so far. They open the system up, they in-

troduce new likenesses, whether it is Shakespeare saying, "My Mistres' eyes are nothing like the Sunne" or it is Newton saying that the moon in essence is exactly like a thrown apple. All those who imagine take parts of the universe which have not been connected hitherto and enlarge the total connectivity of the universe by showing them to be connected.

The creative person, whether scientist or artist, according to Bronowski, is that person who imagines new, different connections, broadening our conception of the universe and its interconnectedness as a whole.

The complete creation of our cosmology, then, must definitely include the model given us by science, this constantly changing and growing model as science itself imagines and discovers new connections. We cannot turn aside from that. But the scientific model must be further enhanced and infused by other human talents and genius, making other new connections. The path to follow, it seems to me, is not contradicting or fighting or turning from science and its beautiful, invigorating story, but assimilating it, incorporating its glory, celebrating both its findings and its method of scrutiny and openness, using its great power and stimulation and beauty as a jumping-off point to an energetic and meaningful spirituality. We are definitely and positively capable of finding and creating spirituality in this cosmology. We have the power and the ability and, possibly, the obligation to do that. We must possess our cosmology rather than being possessed *by* it.

We can begin to do this by making those new imaginative connections and also by examining imaginatively the questions we ask about nature and the universe.

Werner Heisenberg, in *Physics and Philosophy*, states that "natural science does not simply describe and explain nature; it is part of the interplay between nature and ourselves; it describes nature as exposed to our method of questioning."

C. S. Lewis echoes Heisenberg's thought in *The Discarded Image:* "Nature gives most of her evidence in answer to the questions we ask her."

What are the new and startling connections, the innovative questions we may ask of the sycamore leaf, of the wave against the beach, of the raven's call, of the play of a dandelion seed against the sky, of the hands of the lover, of our own involvement in the universe through our observation and delight in these phenomena? We must formulate new questions, ones that will definitely take into account and acknowledge those questions already asked. We must ask questions that accept and incorporate nature's revelations in response to the questions that science asks, but that utilize other realms of investigation, questions that make new connections, new metaphors.

If divinity should rise not from the natural world alone but from our interaction with the natural world, including our interactions with each other, if divinity is created through our manner of bestowing, our reverence, our praise and honor, the gifts we give, and if divinity comes into being likewise through our openness and willingness to receive, then we must ask the questions that allow and encourage these qualities to rise and manifest themselves.

And here's a miracle that must be constantly celebrated: In spite of those moments of the soul's desperation, we do proceed. We do proceed, even in the face of that "unyielding despair" which seems sometimes to be the result of the truths listed by Bertrand Russell. We do continue to attempt to build the soul's habitation. And we do it partially by expressing the awe and thrill and gratitude we feel at the mystery and beauty of the universe as it continues to reveal itself to us through all human disciplines. Being one ourselves with the universe, we continue to create it, to infuse it with meaning, as it continues to reveal and inform us, body and soul. We embrace strongly, as we are in turn embraced by the stars, the heavens, the earth, embraced by the universe through our very revelry in it.

ABOUT THE AUTHORS

CHARLES BAXTER teaches at the University of Michigan and is the author of two novels, *First Light* and *Shadow Play*, as well as three collections of stories: *Harmony of the World*, *Through the Safety Net*, and *A Relative Stranger*. He is the recipient of many grants and awards.

KIMBERLY BLAESER, Anishinabe, writes poetry, short fiction, personal essays, journalism, reviews, and scholarly articles. She is an assistant professor at the University of Wisconsin in Milwaukee.

JOHN MALCOLM BRINNIN is the author of six collections of poetry, including *Selected Poems*, as well as critical studies of Emily Dickinson, William Carlos Williams, and Dylan Thomas, and a biography of Gertrude Stein. He is also an editor, social historian, lecturer, and past director of New York's Poetry Center. Currently a professor emeritus at Boston University, he divides his time between Massachusetts, Italy, and Key West.

KURT BROWN is founding director of the Aspen Writers' Conference, now in its twentieth year, founding director of Writers' Conferences and Festivals (a national association of directors) now in its fifth year, past editor of *Aspen Anthology*, and president of the Aspen Literary Foundation. He is the editor of *The True Subject* (Graywolf Press, 1993) and *Drive, They Said: Poems about Americans and Their Cars* (Milkweed Editions, 1994). His poems have appeared in many literary periodicals. A chapbook, *The Lance and Rita Poems* (co-authored with Virginia Slachman), won the 1994 Sound Post Press competition in Columbia, Missouri (1994). He lives in Snowmass Village, Colorado, and Cambridge, Massachusetts.

ALAN CHEUSE, the author of two short story collections and three novels as well as a memoir, serves as book commentator for National Public Radio's *All Things Considered* as well as host and producer of the NPR Syndicated Fiction Project, *The Sound of Writing*. He teaches in the writing program at George Mason University in Fairfax, Virginia.

STEPHEN COREY has published six collections of poetry: *All These Lands You Call One Country*, *Attacking the Pieta*, *Synchronized Swimming*, *Gentle Iron Lace*, *Fighting Death*, and *The Last Magician*. He has taught at the Universities of Florida and South Carolina, and is currently associate editor of the *Georgia Review*.

HERMAN DE CONINCK is Belgium's leading poet, editor, and critic. He is the author of five highly acclaimed books of poetry in Flemish, two books of critical essays, and is founder and editor of *Nieuw Wereldtijschrift (New World Magazine)* in Antwerp, Belgium.

ALISON DEMING is the director of the Poetry Center at the University of Arizona in Tucson. Her book, *Science and Other Poems*, won the 1993 Walt Whitman Award from the Academy of American Poets and was published by Louisiana State University Press. A collection of her nature essays, *Temporary Homelands*, is available from Mercury House in San Francisco.

BRUCE DUFFY studied English and philosophy at the University of Maryland. In 1988, his essay "The Do-It-Yourself Life of Ludwig Wittgenstein" appeared in the *New York Times Book Review*. His first novel, *The World as I Found It*, is a fictionalized account of Wittgenstein's life. Upon its publication, Anthony Burgess declared it "Book of the Year" on behalf of the London *Observer*.

EDWARD HIRSCH is the author of four books of poems, including *For The Sleepwalkers*, *Wild Gratitude*, *The Night Parade*, and *Earthly Measures*. He teaches in the Creative Writing Program at the University of Houston in Houston, Texas.

LYNDA HULL published two collections of poetry: *Ghost Money*, which won the Juniper Prize at the University of Massachusetts Press in 1986, and *Star Ledger*, which was the winner of the Edwin Ford Piper Poetry Prize from the University of Iowa Press in 1991. She also won four Pushcart Prizes for her poetry and an NEA fellowship. She died in a car accident in 1994. This book is dedicated to her memory.

GARY PAUL NABHAN is an ethnobiologist who spends his time at "Stinkin'" Hot Desert National Monument in Arizona's Sonoran desert. He is the editor of *Counting Sheep: Twenty Ways of Seeing Desert Bighorn*, and the author of *The Desert Smells Like Rain*, a naturalist's study of the ways of the O'odham people.

M. NOURBESE PHILIP's books of poetry include *Thorns, Salmon Courage, She Tries Her Tongue, Her Silence Softly Breaks*, and *Looking for Livingstone: An Odyssey of Silence*. Her novel, *Harriet's Daughter*, was a finalist in 1989 for the Canadian Library Association Prize for Multicultural Literature. She lives in Toronto, Canada.

PATTIANN ROGERS is the author of five books of poetry, including *The Expectations of Light, The Tattooed Lady in the Garden, Legendary Performance, Splitting and Binding*, and *Geocentric*. Winner of many grants and awards for her work, she has taught at the Universities of Texas, Montana, and Arkansas. She currently lives in the foothills of eastern Colorado.

DAVID ST. JOHN has published five books of poetry, including *Hush, The Shore, No Heaven, Terraces of Rain: an Italian Sketchbook*, and *Study for the World's Body: New and Selected Poems*. He has taught at Oberlin College, Johns Hopkins University, and currently teaches at the University of Southern California in Los Angeles. He is the recipient of many grants and awards, most recently the Prix de Rome Fellowship in Literature of the American Academy of Arts and Letters.

EMILY UZENDOSKI received her doctorate in English from the University of Nebraska at Lincoln, and currently teaches at Central Community College in Columbus, Nebraska. Her articles have appeared in journals both in Nebraska and nationally. She is working on a revised annotated bibliography of Nebraska authors, *The Nebraska Authors Data Base*, for which she received a grant.

RUTH WHITMAN is the author of many books of poems, including *Laughing Gas: Poems New and Selected 1963–1990, Permanent Address: New Poems 1973–1980, The Passion of Lizzie Borden: New and Selected Poems*, and *Tamsen Donner: A Woman's Journey*. An essayist and teacher, she has written and narrated a television documentary and helped to translate, with others, the works of I. B. Singer, Alain Bosquet, Abraham Sutzkever, and Jacob Glatstein.

DAVID WOJAHN has published four collections of poetry: *Icehouse Lights*, which won the Yale Series of Younger Poets Award in 1981, *Glassworks, Mystery Train*, and *Late Empire*, all from the University of Pittsburgh Press. He has taught at the University of New Orleans and the University of Arkansas, and is currently teaching at Indiana University in Bloomington.

ACKNOWLEDGMENTS

Excerpt from Edward Abbey is from his *The Journey Home*, published by E. P. Dutton. Copyright © 1977 by Edward Abbey.

Excerpts from Donald Barthelme are from "Not Knowing," which first appeared in *Gulf Coast*, vol. 4, no. 1, 1990.

Charles Baxter, "Talking Forks: Fiction and the Inner Life of Objects," first appeared in the *Gettysburg Review*, vol. 6, no. 1, Winter 1993.

Elizabeth Bishop, *Questions of Travel* is published by Farrar, Straus & Giroux. Copyright © 1952, 1965 by Elizabeth Bishop. Excerpts from Elizabeth Bishop, "Over 2,000 Illustrations and a Complete Concordance," are from *The Complete Poems, 1927–1979*, by Elizabeth Bishop. Copyright © 1979, 1983 by Alice Helen Methfessel. Reprinted by permission of Farrar, Straus & Giroux, Inc.

Kimberly M. Blaeser, "Entering the Canon: Our Place in World Literature," first appeared in *Akwe:kon* ("All of Us"), a Journal of Indigenous Issues, vol. 10, no. 1, Spring 1993.

Excerpt from Richard Brautigan is from his *So the Wind Won't Blow It All Away*, published by Delacourt/Seymour Lawrence. Copyright © 1932 by Richard Brautigan.

John Malcolm Brinnin, "Travel and the Sense of Wonder," was first published as a chapbook, in the Viewpoint Series, no. 29, by the Florida Center for the Book and the Center for the Book in the Library of Congress, 1992.

Excerpt from Jacob Bronowski is from his *The Origin of Knowledge and Imagination*, published by Yale University Press. Copyright © 1978 by Yale University.

Excerpt from Stephen Corey, "Three Poems," is reprinted by permission of Stephen Corey. Copyright © 1993 by Stephen Corey. "'She is startled at the big sound': Poetry as Translation," by Stephen Corey, first appeared in the *Laurel Review*, Winter 1994.

Excerpts from E. E. Cummings, "anyone lived in a pretty how town" and "what if a much of a which of a wind," are from *Complete Poems, 1904–1962*, by E. E. Cummings, edited by George J. Firmage. Reprinted by permission of Liveright Publish-